Be the Successor

Strong Habits of Life and Business

JASON ALLEN

Published by SuburbanBuzz.com LLC

ISBN: 978-1-959446-17-0

DEDICATION

This book is dedicated to my wife, Kathy, who inspired me to be the best I can be, taught me to see the best in everyone, and stood by me through everything.

A special thanks goes out to my family-—Jacob for being my first experience as a father, Tyson for being a leader, Brazos for his unparalleled strength, Kamdon for being a dreamer, Beckett for being the witty entertainer, Sofia for being the creative perfectionist, Hudson for his kind heart, and Maris for being the little princess. The only thing more rewarding than completing this book is getting to share it with all of you.

CONTENTS

ACKNOWLEDGMENTS

After more than five long years of working on Be the Successor, we have finally come to a conclusion. The years have come with my trials and tribulations that both added creative fuel for what you have read, as well as distractions which caused me to spend more than five years writing it.

Over the course of its conception, there are many people who deserve to be recognized for their contributions. Those who were not listed in the book, nor specifically in the acknowledgements, please note that your contributions did not go unnoticed.

First and foremost, I would like to acknowledge my family for their unwavering support and encouragement throughout the entire process. I would also like to acknowledge my circles for their unique contributions, valuable insights and continued motivation. My editor, Melanie Saxton, deserves a special thanks for pushing me to get through the last 25% of the book. You provided so much guidance and constructive feedback, which allowed me to get to this astounding, completed product. My publisher, Holly Chervnsik of SuburbanBuzz Publishing, gave my work a face with your well-designed cover and brought my work to life by putting it all together.

I want to thank everyone who beta read the book and provided constructive feedback and provided direction for where parts of the book should go. I appreciate everyone in the ProActive office for keeping the machine running while I was frequently preoccupied with the book. The readers and supporters who have been eagerly anticipating this work – your enthusiasm kept me going. This book would not have been possible without the collective efforts and support of these amazing individuals. Thank you for being a part of this journey.

INTRODUCTION TO EVOLUTION

In this introduction, I'm not going to tell you where I've come from. I'll let you figure that out throughout this book. I will say where I'm going and exactly how I'm going to get there.

What does it mean to be "the successor?" It means that you're the next in line. It is now your time. What you're about to inherit throughout this book are strong habits that will usher you to the front of the line. The line is out the door and around the corner with competitive individuals who strive to be just as hungry as you are, so let's get the edge on them, shall we?

I am not here to tell you the secret way to success because it isn't a secret at all. I am here to do exactly what the subtitle of the book suggests—provide you with strong habits that will help build a foundation of success in your life, as well as in business. However, it is your choice to apply them. All those who are successful know it's directly related to the amount of work you put in. Your journey will not flow with a downhill current. You'll be traveling upstream and will have to paddle your ass off to get where you want to be. Not only are we fighting the discouraging current that flows hard against us, but we also must be aware of rocky terrain and other obstacles that may detour our course to success.

This book is written conversationally. It's meant to be easy to read and combines common sense with strategies for personal and professional growth. It provides an astute overview with real-life examples of what and what not to do. After all, the challenging terrain mentioned above is a fact of life. Overcoming is the goal, as painlessly as possible. Make it a priority to spend your energy creating paths that run seamlessly around your rocky adversaries. The river will always find a way around the rocks in its way; it just depends on how you view the rocks and what you decide to do with them. If you view them as a problem, could you change your mindset and see them as simply an adventure? Can you see yourself as the river, with nothing capable of stopping your current from flowing freely?

You'll notice that many of the topics covered in this book are built on familiar concepts. Everything in this world is built on a concept. There are not as many new ideas as there are new perspectives on existing concepts. I am hopeful that when you finish reading this book, you'll walk away with a different mindset (or understanding) with extra ideas in your toolbox. More so, I want you to view problems with new knowledge of how to remedy, reverse, and recover in ways you haven't considered before.

These concepts will encourage the winning mindset that sets us apart from the rest of the crowd.

Something I often hear from those around me is their awareness of me constantly keeping busy and always doing *something*, and they're absolutely right. I am constantly pulling rocks from my river so the current can flow freely and smoothly. I will never stop until I get to where I intend to go, and I have made it to the mountaintop. But even then, I won't be satisfied with my journey. The end goal for me is not just to reach the mountaintop. It is simply a time for me to reflect on my journey and subsequently look for new mountains to climb. What truly makes great entrepreneurs is not sitting content at the summit of their achievements but rather having the ability to see higher mountains to climb in the distance. This is the point that gives you a clear view of where you want to go and the best path to take to get there. Now is the time to decide what this means for you.

There will undoubtedly be times when you fall off the productive wagon, but that's what evolution is about. How can you pick yourself up and adapt to the situation? How can you respond more appropriately? The topics covered throughout the book are to bring to light a number of frequently overlooked keys to success—minuscule details that you often take for granted.

Foster these ideas and nurture them as your own. This level of confidence will allow you to produce substantial gains. You're the only one who can make a difference and promote greatness in your own life. That fight can only come from within you.

The worst thing that you can do is read this book and not apply the habits I've laid out for you. If that is you, then put this book down and go back to living the life that made you pick it up in the first place. When writing this book, I immediately stopped what I was doing to write what I felt as soon as I felt it, whether I was mowing the lawn, sitting with colleagues at happy hour, or running on the treadmill. When inspiration struck, I ran with it. These sparks of inspiration are what motivated me to keep going, and it's my responsibility to relay them in a fashion that motivates you. Each chapter is a stand-alone concept that is meant to be independently thought-provoking while systematically building a better you.

My writing style is very abstract. I could be working on a certain chapter one day and bounce back five chapters to add something that moved me the next day. It is my expectation that you do the same. Refer back, add your own content, apply your own experiences, and decide what will personally elevate you the most. Completely defile this book's margins with your own notes, dog ears, and Post-It notes. Each chapter is meant to be independently thought-provoking while systematically building a better you. Whatever time you need to better yourself, take that time. This is all about you; I am only here to motivate you to step out of your shell, become who you know you can be, and facilitate your success.

This book gives you the tools to be successful, but the *key* to success lies within you. There is no specific entrepreneurial DNA that automatically destines you to be a success. You must take what is yours. What does your end game look like to you? In your view, does it come from a cushioned bank account, social media likes, appealing aesthetics, or materialistic and continually depreciating items? These are all tangible objects or traits that can, of course, assist you on your journey, but what is the sole intangible that should trump all others?

Your will to win. That's the *intangible* that matters. Are you putting in the reps? Are you gritting out the early mornings? Are you struggling through the late nights? These are all intangibles that are necessary to achieve the dream. If you don't dream about being the best, then what's the point in dreaming? You're the only one who can choose your level of success, and if you believe in something long enough, it will manifest itself into reality. Whether good or bad, it will come to fruition.

The power of thought is just that…a power. A superpower, really. You can have all the potential in the world and an exorbitant amount of money. But without the will to win and elevate your life, you will, without a doubt, sit idle. There are no participation trophies in business or in life. You either win, or you don't. You either meet your goals, or you don't.

Like I tell my kids, look outward, not downward. When I was teaching them how to ride their bikes, I told them to look out at what was in front of them and not at their feet. You know where your feet are. Looking out front allows you to see what's ahead and helps you know where you're going. Knowing where you're going is what makes a winner.

Do you believe yourself to be a winner? Those who fail to exhibit the trait of this intangible will hover at the bottom, rocking your podium in an attempt to shake you off balance. The intangible to win is the one thing that maintains your balance.

The process of writing this book has undoubtedly been a long and tedious journey for me. Since its conception, a number of ideologies that were planned for the book were tossed aside. I am not the person I was when I first started plotting the outline. My evolution as a husband, a father, a chiropractor, a business owner, an entrepreneur, and wholly as a human being has gone through vast changes.

The special part is that I, like you, will continue to constantly evolve. My goals have changed, my perception of those goals has changed, and my process of attaining those goals has changed, always pushing me to evolve for a better tomorrow.

CHAPTER 1
THE WINNING MINDSET

Every battle is won before it is fought.

~ Sun Tzu

As I stare at myself intently, I'm analyzing every contour of my face, every blemish. I notice the bead of sweat that has initiated its way down the left side of my face. My breathing is heavy. My fists are clenched as they rest on the vanity. My arms are trembling as I attempt to support my weight. There's a knock at the door.

"Five minutes until you go on stage!" my manager yells. The sweat increasingly pours down my face. This will be my first time speaking to such a large audience. *Who would appoint me the keynote speaker of such a large event?* It feels as if the stage lights are already beaming down on me. I can literally feel the heat consuming my body.

What if I completely forget what to say? What if I fumble over my words? What if they get up and walk out? What if they boo me off the stage? While these are all valid concerns, they have no bearing on the amount of preparation I have put in to be here. I lean into the mirror to take a closer look. My breath fogs it up, blurring this nervous version of myself. I grab the towel sitting on the counter to wipe the fog away, and in this moment, see myself differently. I know these are merely insecurities in the wake of a new venture. I know I've put in the work to get to this point, and it's my time to share it with the world. I affirm the fact that these people are here because they believe in my work. They value what I have to say, and they want to hear more.

I got this! My fists lift slightly off the counter and immediately come

5

back down with a resounding thud. *I got this!* I confidently say to myself and take one last deep breath. I grab my notes from the coffee table in the middle of the dressing room, and I make my way to the side stage to await my introduction. From where I'm standing left of the stage, I can see the crowd eager to be inspired. The host speaker begins the build-up of my introduction, but to me, it's muffled. My head is filled with the imagery of every step that was taken to get to this point. I can feel the constant light patting of my notes against my thigh as I wait in the wings. Then it all becomes clear.

"And your keynote speaker, Jason Allen!"

I don't know how many deep breaths I took at that moment, but my chest was puffed up, and I felt ten feet tall. I made my way to the center of the stage and knocked it out of the park.

This is a scenario I've had many times with myself. We've all been there, in one way or another, talking to ourselves in that metaphorical mirror. It's this recurring talk about our mental approach regarding ourselves, times in our lives, and situations that present themselves to us. During this time, we take a personal inventory of what has allowed us to be successful. They are the attributes that set us apart from the rest of the crowd. They are the attributes that make up the winner's mindset.

A person's mindset is the key to all success. It's the one thing that can/will make you or break you. A winner cannot be defined by money, success, fame, accolades, or popularity. It's about how we perceive ourselves, how we project that onto others, and how we take ownership of our own losses. A winner's mindset is the intangible that makes them a winner. When you have acquired this mindset, you have the ability to have tunnel vision. This tunnel vision of your goal brings awareness of what enters your peripheral. The details of the task become precisely clear, and you're able to tackle them with extreme focus. You cannot be shaken.

The Intangibles

How can your intangibles empower your tangible assets? If your assets revolve around physicality, then put in the work, get in the gym, pound the pavement, and make it work. If you don't reach your goal to be the best or you don't win the championship, then it's back to the drawing board, and you figure it out. Whether you're on the ground floor, a middle manager, or a C-suite executive, there's a level of determination you must have to call yourself a winner. That level only goes up when you strive to achieve with the elite of the elite. If you're repeatedly achieving your goals, that's great! Are your goals high enough? Are you setting "elite status" goals, or are you setting modest benchmarks that you know you can reach?

I'm a big Tim Tebow fan, if only for the simple fact that he is a winner. If you put him in a tough situation, he'll make it a winning situation. From before birth, Tim, or his mother rather, faced circumstances that only the truly strong survive. While on a mission trip in the Philippines, his mother conceived her fifth child while seriously ill with amoebic dysentery. Pam Tebow was immediately advised to abort the pregnancy as it was a danger to her survival, and the doctors claimed it wasn't even a baby but only a mass of fetal tissue.

When the doctor delivered "Timmy the Tumor," as his siblings jokingly called him, he said it was "the biggest miracle he had ever been a part of" and "he had never seen anything like it, and he couldn't explain it." For anyone who doesn't know the ins and outs of pregnancy, a baby survives fully enclosed inside of a placenta. When Tebow was born, there was just a tiny piece of placenta attached to him and "no explanation for how he survived all those months in the womb," according to Mrs. Tebow's doctor. You can read more about his background and incredible life thus far in his insightful book *This is The Day* and *Through My Eyes*.

I simply want to supply a superior demonstration of what it means to be a winner. As mentioned earlier, you can have all the tangible qualities in the world, but if you can't utilize them, they are worthless. There are so many other guys who have more size, speed, and power than Tim Tebow but lack the intangible of being a winner.

Both on and off the field, Tim was faced with relentless critics, telling him that he was not good enough or his faith was not meant for the football field. In the end, he won national championships. He won the Heisman Trophy. He achieved his goal of starting as a quarterback in the NFL, and his faith has never been broken. He emerged as a winner. Although his football career was cut short and was arguably less than glamorous, he was able to adapt to the obstacles that life threw at him, transitioning to broadcasting and eventually pursuing a career in professional baseball. Along with his will to win, Tim uses many of the habits that are emphasized in this book, such as making the right decisions, having the enticing confidence to overcome obstacles, being a problem solver, and putting things into perspective, just to name a few.

The intangible is being a winner. That is what having a winning mindset is about. You're the first to arrive, the last to leave, and always pushing for that extra rep. You recognize your accomplishments but realize you can do more to create a better life. And life will undoubtedly punch you in the face from time to time. Sure, some people are going to lose more teeth than others, but the ones who have the mental toughness to get back up are the ones who prosper. When shit gets hard, you do not curl up in a fetal position and hope that someone is going to save you. It's about who can take the punches, get back up, go back to the drawing board, and put together a plan to succeed. It's the ongoing mentality of *I'm going to do twice as much work as last year and half as much the next.* This is what sets the winners apart from the rest of the pack.

Doing The Gritty

At 35 years old, just following the divorce from my first wife, I decided it was time to mark off some of the items on my bucket list and start living. As is most people's list, mine contained the typical entries like skydiving and traveling to numerous locations around the world. However, sitting at the top of my list was "Compete in an MMA fight." After 13 years removed from wrestling in college and well passed my athletic prime, I decided to sign up for a fight. At this point, I had minimal jiujitsu experience, practically zero stand-up, and would be relying very heavily on my very dusty wrestling experience. Only 13 years out. It's like riding a bike, though, right?

Just after the start of the new year, I told my coach, who was also a regional promoter, that I wanted to compete on the April fight card. His response was simply, "Dude, you're fat and out of shape." I was adamant and stayed my course in the gym. If it wasn't going to be the April card, I would look again to the Fall. A week went by, and he walked up to me after practice one evening and asked if I would still like to compete in April. I jumped on the opportunity, and we got to work. In the four months of my fight camp, I lost thirty-five pounds to get to fight weight, put together a game plan, and got myself into shape.

Two weeks before the fight, my opponent pulled out, and we scrambled to find a replacement. After a week of searching, we found a fighter whose opponent also pulled out last minute before his fight in Houston. There was only one catch—he was a weight class below me, and I agreed to fight at a catchweight. This meant that I had to lose an additional five pounds.

In the final days leading up to the fight, I was extremely tired from a calorie deficit, dehydrated as I had begun to cut my water intake, and mentally exhausted from hours in the sauna to drop off the last little bit of weight leading up to weigh-ins.

One of my teammates, Ellis, chauffeured me from the gym to a local hotel where the formal weigh-ins took place. All the fighters sat in the lobby looking depleted but still sizing each other up and waiting for their time to step on the scale. After a few fighters had gone back, my opponent and I were called back for our official weights. As I waited for him to get weighed in, I stared eagerly at the Pedialyte and banana in my teammate's hands. Finally, I stepped on the scale. It read 179.5. I was a half-pound under the limit. I immediately stepped off the scale, began rehydrating, and off to Texas Roadhouse we went to fully replenish.

The next day was fight day. Ellis picked me up from the house and drove me to the venue. During the commute, he had me cue up a video. It was a video of Will Smith talking about facing his fear of skydiving. Will told a story about how he faced his fear of skydiving with a group of friends in Dubai. He discussed the process of the flight and how scared he was leading up to the jump. "Was I scared? Hell, yes, I was scared," he said.

As I watched the video, I began to calm myself. And then Will said this: "On the other side of your maximum fear are all of the best things in life." If you're searching for a sharp and profound motto, that's it.

We arrived at the venue a few hours before the start of the event for the rules meeting and an opportunity to examine the cage. I stood in the back, waiting for my coach to walk out to the cage, when I peered through the curtain and saw my opponent in the cage. He shuffled around and threw numerous spinning kicks. I could only imagine he was picturing me standing in front of him. I thought to myself, *Shit, I'm about to get my head kicked off in front of all my friends.*

When fight time came, I made my way to the cage where he was already standing. My adrenaline was so spiked that my energy level was already depleted by about half before I even stepped into the cage. It was time. The cage door was shut behind me, the bell rang, we touched gloves, and it was on. I scored takedowns in the first two rounds and maintained control for the duration of those rounds. Winning both of those rounds decisively, I knew all I had to do was get through the last round and not get knocked out. When the bell rang to come out for the third round, I could barely stand. He could see from across the way that I was exhausted, and he quickly made his way toward me, not giving me a chance to catch my breath. We began circling each other before we both started throwing strikes…and then it happened. He hit me with a left-hand right on the button, and I went down to the canvas.

I woke up lying face down and thought, *What happened? Why am I on the mat? Is the fight over?* Right then, he began punching me in the side of the face. I saw his legs planted around my head as he continued raining down punches. I instinctively grabbed onto one of his legs in an attempt to neutralize the situation. At this moment, I switched into survival mode, pinning up against the fence, holding on to his leg for dear life, and trying to regain my composure. I had to grit out this last round to get the win. He smelled blood in the water and landed 45 unanswered punches to my head before I was finally able to change my angle and take him down, where I held him for the remainder of the match.

The final bell rang, and I slowly stood up in a level of exhaustion that I had never experienced before. We stood there in the center of the cage with the referee between us, anticipating the final decision. The winner was announced, and I stood there in a sea of chanting fans with my arms raised.

The point of the story is this. In life, you're going to get knocked to the ground repeatedly. There are going to be times when you get punched 45 fucking times in the face with little chance to recover, but you sure as hell can't stay down. Your only option is to have the grit to get back on your feet and continue to fight.

Promoted to blue belt in BJJ by my coach Bubba Bush.

Face off with my opponent at weigh ins the night before my MMA fight.

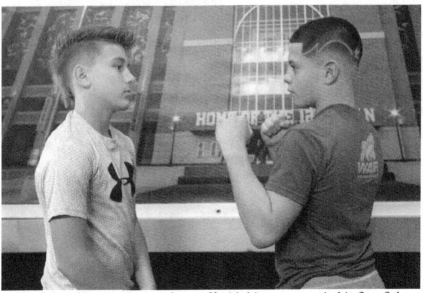

Like father, like son. Brazos faces off with his opponent in his first fight.

Channeling Your Mental Game

I truly found my balance when I met my wife, Kathy. She brought something to my life that had never been present before and that allowed me to wholeheartedly commit to greatness in all facets of my life. Where I always had the grit to press forward, there were many times that I lacked the finesse to really hone into some of my greater attributes. I've always been the train on the tracks, full speed ahead, and there was no stopping me. There were many times when I was chugging along with no station in sight. When Kathy came into my life, she almost acted as the conductor, stoking the fire, getting me down the track, and stopping me at the most productive stations.

With that being said, it wasn't until Kathy and I kicked off our Workshop Wednesdays that I really felt that urge. Workshop Wednesdays started as three-hour morning periods we time-blocked and discussed our goals. Our goal was, and is, simply to streamline our success. We created a timeline of each of our goals, short, mid, and long-term so that they would snowball from one to the next.

I couldn't wait for Wednesdays to come around. I yearned for those weekly creative explosions. I jotted down notes throughout the week and counted down the days until I got to throw them on the table. Sure, we talked about ideas on other days as well, but Wednesday was the day that we really got in-depth about everything. It allowed me to express myself through my creativity and my entrepreneurial spirit. Our workshops evolved into six to seven-hour think tanks, with just us and also our colleagues. The return on investment was greater during that productive window than it would have been seeing patients in the office. It allowed me to set things up in order to build an empire.

Our goal was to build something we both loved; a prosperous life full of successful businesses, an abundance of passive money streams, a happy family with plenty of travel, and spending time with the kids. We must love what we do. If the love is not there, then the will to win won't be there. Without love, you'll merely see obstacles that you must overcome to succeed as opportunities to quit. I like the phrase "Make your vocation your vacation," meaning we should never look at our work as an obligation.

Let's just say the average person works for 45 years. They start working around 20 years old and retire at the average age of 65. The average life expectancy in the developed world, on the high end, is 80 years. This means that over half of your life is spent working. You better love what you do, or you're cheating yourself. You should always love being in the "office" and never dread going back to work on Monday morning.

While this statement is true, it's also assuming that you're already there, that you've already made it. Life is a progression of one experience to the next, with our loves and objectives ever-changing. I enjoy what I do in my office, but like anything else in life, it has its ups and downs. I love helping people, I love interacting with people, and I love the stability of it. I don't dread Mondays, and I don't anticipate the weekends because I know that each day I'm at work is just another opportunity for me to make more money, another moment to help those I interact with, and another chance to build my brand.

I wanted to take the previous quote a step further and say, "Affinity to infinity." Find that one thing that draws you in, the one thing that ignites your whole being, and grab on. Hold fast to that one thing that drives you from the moment you get out of bed in the morning and never let go. That is your passion! This is the intangible that pushes you to an optimal mindset of productivity and creativity. Your success lies there.

So, what is success to you? However you choose to answer the question, the road to get there remains constant. The habits are universal and apply to all walks of life, professional and personal. To me, a winner's mindset is getting to the end of life and knowing you gave it all. There was not one mountain that you set out to climb that you did not summit. Once you grasp this mindset, you can grasp any opportunity.

The Choice Is Yours

I sent a raw version of what you've read in this chapter to my nephew, Tyler, who was going through basic training in the Army. Throughout the first weeks of training, before the commencement of hard physical training, he would write or call home and share how mentally testing it was. He was the youngest in his platoon and it was his first time living away from home. Within weeks, some could not take it and had fallen out. He began to get nervous about what was in store for the remainder of the training. I relayed to him something I learned in my years of strenuous conditioning for wrestling and MMA; your mind will give up on you way before your body will.

A couple of months into his training, I wrote a handwritten note to remind him to be mindful of the beauty of the autumn leaves changing to all shades of reds and oranges and reminded him that we were all proud of him. Then I typed out the chapter, sent it up to Fort Leonard Wood in a manilla envelope, and waited anxiously for his reply, like a little kid checking the mail for a letter from a pen pal. Finally, he wrote back to me and let me know how much he enjoyed it and that it motivated him to keep pressing on. He said he passed it around to the other guys in the bunk to look over and even had the lead sergeant read it.

He said that many of the guys had different responses and mindsets regarding the passage. Some were motivated by what they had read, some questioned their own mindset, and others wondered why someone was even sending them a book chapter in the first place. All of these are valid responses, and they show whose mindset would allow them to succeed. When I sent my follow up letter, I simply explained, "some people have the mindset to lead the platoon and others have the mindset to fall in line. The choice is yours."

Tyler reaching for the top during basic training.

CHAPTER 2
THE SHOPPING CART

We are a product of the choices we make, not the circumstances that we face.

~ Roger Crawford

During my ten years as a personal trainer, I found myself making a game out of analyzing people's shopping carts in the grocery store. I would try to understand what kind of person they were by what foods or items were in their carts. Obviously, I couldn't go up to the person and ask them what their life was like, but I felt I could observe and make superficial assumptions about how they were choosing to live their lives by doing so. More often than not, what they had in their shopping cart was a direct reflection of their appearance, and what I could only assume was how they lived their day-to-day life.

What can I say? It was my job as a personal trainer to observe people's habits and tie them to their overall health and wellness. Generally, the shopping carts filled with frozen pizzas, sodas, candy, chips, and mounds of processed foods belonged to someone who was overweight and seemingly unhealthy or just your typical college student shopping on the "Ramen Noodle and hot dog" budget. On the flip side, the shopping carts filled with fresh fruits and veggies, lean meats and bottled waters were directly correlated to someone with what appeared to be a healthy lifestyle. Not only did this group look healthier, but they moved about much easier, with greater confidence, almost like they were able to shift into another gear.

I remember a specific day when I noticed a man two aisles away as I was walking to check out. There he stood, attempting to make a life change but not completely sure of how to do it. His cart was filled with Lean Cuisine meals, reduced fat treats for their midnight snacking and Crystal Light drink packets because they "hate the taste of water." Commendably, they had made the decision to incorporate these changes to better their lifestyles, but what they needed was simply some guidance to enrich the potential benefits in each of their new decision-making endeavors.

The shopping cart game would eventually become habit forming. I couldn't help but analyze every person that I crossed paths with in the grocery store aisles. As our opposing paths intersected, I would intently examine the items in their cart to determine my preliminary analysis.

After playing the game for a while, it began to develop more depth. I started to ask myself, "What kinds of decisions do these people make to fill their shopping carts with these types of items?" I didn't mean decisions like, "Hmm, do I want white or wheat bread?" or even, "Do I want to be healthy and get the grilled chicken or should I get these Hot Pockets because they're on sale?" I am talking about really digging in deep as to how these people got here. I thought about the person with the mounds of processed foods and sugary junk in their cart. Why did they make the choice to purchase this food, knowing how unhealthy it was for them? Were they shopping on a budget due to financial burdens and convenience, or were the choices made because they didn't care about their body?

If these choices were actually due to finances, were they prioritizing their budget on activities such as drinking or smoking that put them in that position? Do they shop this way to allow for those *other* unhealthy lifestyle choices? I am not critiquing anyone's lifestyle but rather stating that, simply put, everyone's decisions directly influence the next step in their life. It's somewhat of a chicken-and-egg-type situation. Our lives are all about the decisions we make each day, both big and small, and provide the infrastructure that will determine our rate of growth. These decisions are ultimately what do or **don't** allow us to end up at our desired destination.

John

Let's take a look at our first scenario with a man we'll call "John." Standing behind his cart, John is blatantly dissatisfied with himself. The slouch in his back personifies the numerous tallies he has accrued in life's loss column, and his scruffy neck beard screams, "Shaving once a week is plenty for me." His clothes look nice but are clearly a little tighter than they were a few years ago when he sported the athletic physique of his football glory days.

Looking back, John grew up as an average guy in a middle-upper-class home and had things handed to him throughout his youth. By the time he entered high school, he was on the Varsity football team, and although John rarely went to class, he excelled enough in sports that he was often given a free pass. John earned a partial scholarship to play football in college but continued with this same negligent behavior. He was living in the dorms and using his meal plan to eat in the school cafeteria, which meant he could use his monthly budget from his parents to splurge on junk food and booze. He had to get the full college experience, right? Well, before he knew it, the party life began to take priority over academics, and he slid down the slippery slope of skipping classes just like he did in high school.

Preceding a Friday football practice, the coach announced that the players would have to run one hill for every absence they incurred that week, in addition to the scheduled workout. The coach could only moderate the pace of John's descent for so long. His athletics had also begun to spiral downward on top of his already declining academics. Soon after, the social aspect of college also took precedence over football. He contemplated quitting the team, but his parents assured him that that would be a regretful decision. Ultimately though, it was John's decision, and he made up his mind. He quit the team! It wasn't long after the next spring semester started, and he was already over the allotted amount of absences.

Lacking the structure of spring ball and offseason conditioning, there was nothing to regulate his social life. It was quickly apparent that John was not mature enough to manage himself without some sort of parental guidance or governing mechanism. He was called into the Dean's office and dismissed from the college, which meant any money paid towards the semester went straight down the drain. John waited out the summer as he had decided to reapply to the same school. Although there was joy to be had in being readmitted to the college, the decisions that led to his expulsion continued to linger, throwing off his rhythm. His motivation diminished, and halfway through the fall semester, he withdrew from his classes. Wanting to keep up with his preferred lifestyle, John began to bartend in the evenings. His decision was to make money now rather than later (a topic that we'll cover in

Brick by Brick).

John was now making a very average income but spending it on unhealthy habits, not necessities. There was an obvious need for him to stretch what little money he had, which left him sleeping on friends' couches or having to split the rent with multiple roommates. The silver lining in this chapter is that he learned the great skill of survival.

Now, let's get back to him standing in the grocery store. John was never able to save money to buy a home. He worked incessantly to make ends meet and was worn down, fatigued, and flat-out exhausted. He appears to be an average guy in his thirties, just trying to claw his way out of the hole that he dug for himself. What sits in John's cart directly reflects who he is—he shops for convenience while staying within his budget. Peering into his cart, there are boxed dinners and on-the-go snacks, giving him the option to quickly and with total disregard for nutrition, fill his stomach and get back to his favorite TV show or sporting event. The six-pack of beer sitting in his cart says he still drinks but is trying to keep it under control due to the hangovers lasting a little longer than they did in his twenties. I notice some lean meat and vegetables tossed throughout the cart, which tells me he often reminisces about the life he once had. I can see he is holding on to the slight hope that he might rekindle some motivation to get himself back into shape. Finally, from beneath the other items in his cart peaks a mid-sized container of off-brand coffee, which says that he needs something to get him through the day and "This will work just as good as the gourmet brands."

Some people may ask, "How can you make assumptions about a person based on what is in the cart?" I can make these assumptions because that was once me. I was a late bloomer (nearing thirty years old) learning how to "shop" for a better life for myself. I wanted everything now, to have fun and experience the world, and I did. I created memories that would have you rolling on the floor laughing your ass off for days, but I couldn't buy a house or a car. I traveled around this country (and to a few others) but couldn't get rid of the stress that came from living paycheck to paycheck. I went to hundreds of concerts and drank many nights away, but I couldn't put money back to get ahead. It took a long time, but the hole began to get shallower and the world began to get brighter.

Looking back on everything I had done, I can't believe that I was so irresponsible with my finances. Was everything I experienced worth all of the headache/heartache that had accrued over those 10-15 years? Not even close! If I had dug down early, then I would have bypassed a lot of the issues which set me back, and I could have created more extravagant experiences a decade later. We'll touch on this in the next chapter, *The Dopamine Response*, but the sooner you can balance the "now vs. later" battle in your head, the sooner you'll reach a higher level of success.

Lucy

Standing in line behind John is a young woman, seemingly in her mid-twenties. Let's call her Lucy. As Lucy pushes her cart into the line, John can't help but notice her messy hair and the look of complete exhaustion on her face. There's a toddler on her hip, and she's wearing a loose-fitting dress, attempting to conceal a second-trimester baby bump. She gently pats the child's thigh with her left hand, revealing a small and modest engagement band. The ring indicates that she is content with whatever her future spouse can give her, even though her posture says that she is frustrated with the direction her life has taken her up to this point. However, there's a look about her that hints she has the determination to get herself and her family on the right path.

John looks into her cart, and it's full of Mac and Cheese, hot dogs, fish sticks, cereal, and prepackaged meals she can quickly throw together for herself. She shops for convenience and to provide for her child, all the while selflessly neglecting her own health and happiness. Lucy, a newly engaged mom, works multiple jobs with little time to cook. Her grocery shopping is dictated by the choices she made that landed her where she is today. She reaches the register and swipes her debit card, fully prepared for it to decline due to insufficient funds.

What decisions did she make to get herself here? Why is she so nervous in an attempt to feed her family?

Lucy grew up in a mid-sized town and was friends with everyone. She was a people pleaser, concerned with being liked by everyone. What Lucy lacked was self-worth. She desperately needed to like herself, her choices, and the results. But with every failed relationship and every failed attempt to become the person she wanted to be, she sought out comfort from the wrong partner. She didn't want to be alone. She didn't want to feel alone. And so, she initially settled.

At the age of 22, Lucy fell pregnant with her first child by a man who had no intention of sticking around. Being a single parent, she was forced to quit college and get a job to provide for herself and her baby. Throughout the pregnancy, she overcame extreme fatigue to work as much as she could before giving birth. When her baby boy finally arrived, she took time off from work to bond with him. Lucy did not work at a job that offered paid maternity leave, so her savings quickly dwindled. Following an involuntary shortened leave, she returned to work with the addition of a second job to compensate for another mouth to feed.

Lucy is still working those two jobs but met a nice man who stepped up to be a father figure to her son. He married her and blessed her with another child. Through her hard work, she has been able to gain some pride in her life which allowed her to choose a suitor that was more accommodating to her needs rather than his own. She began to make decisions that should bring her life back to a place of stability. Lucy has been faced with a number of obstacles that have created detours in her life, but she has shown much resilience to allow herself to get back on track.

Just as I made the assumption of John, I made the same assumption with Lucy because this, too, was my life. I had my first child at 22 years old, got married, and had to work multiple jobs to make ends meet. Even working multiple jobs, I can't begin to count the times I wrote a check hoping it would float me for a few days, because I simply didn't have the money to make it to payday. I can remember the tight, nervous pit in my stomach and sweaty palms as I swiped my card, knowing damn good and well the purchase may not clear and I'd be left with the unbearable shame from the judgment of others waiting in line behind me.

I remarried, had more kids, and still lived paycheck to paycheck well into my thirties. We floated money in and out of our account, budgeting to get groceries, worrying about utilities being shut off, and living in constant angst. With all of this stress and frustration, I made the conscious decision to go back to school and become a chiropractor. I mean, I might as well rack up another $300,000 in debt, no biggie.

When I started school, I only had two children, an eight-year-old and a one-year-old. By the time I graduated from doctorate school, I had four children. The school's academic calendar ran on a trimester program which meant year-round school. We averaged 25-28 credit hours per trimester, but there was a specific trimester I took a whopping 33 credit hours.

If you aren't familiar with the average number of credit hours for a college, most universities cap you at 18 hours. We were slammed with nearly double that number of upper-level science courses. On top of all this, I owned my own personal training business and went to clients' houses for in-home training. For four years, my schedule was grueling. My mornings started at 4:30 to allow me to get out of the house by 5:00 and to my client's house by 5:30. I'd swing by a coffee shop for maybe 30 minutes to get a cup of Joe before school, spend nine long hours on campus (7:30 a.m.–4:30 p.m.), and then try to squeeze my own workouts into a one or two-hour gap in my schedule.

This was how my schedule looked pretty much daily. Working out with my only free time was the last thing I wanted to do, but nobody wants an out-of-shape trainer. Following school, I went back to training, sometimes until 9 p.m., and rarely got to see or spend time with my kids. If I had an exam scheduled for the next day, I'd start studying by 9:30 p.m. and get as much in as my body and mind could tolerate.

I was a nontraditional student in my thirties with exponentially more responsibilities than my peers. I remember a classmate coming up to me one day and saying, "I don't know how you do it, man. I struggle to get by, and I'm single with no kids. You work, have a wife, and four kids. That's crazy!"

This is because I made a conscious decision not to fail. Failing was never and will never be an option. Never, at any point throughout my time in the doctorate program, did quitting outweigh the ability to provide for my children and to build something that they could be a part of. I would never change the fact that I had my boys when I did; they are the best part of me.

However, I have wondered how the decision to have my children so early has affected my life. Having Jacob so young definitely brought a financial strain into my life that I had never experienced before. This, on top of being a single parent, brought on emotional and mental stress as well. I often wondered, as a guy in my twenties, if my "stock had dropped." *Would I be more patient if I had allowed my career to blossom first before becoming a parent?*

I definitely plan to advise my children to establish themselves as their own people before taking on a partner or having a child. You're not a magnet; like attracts like. If you're broken and unstable, then you'll attract broken and unstable people. If you're established and driven, you'll attract established and driven people. Regardless, Lucy's decisions were made, and the path was paved. Her decisions set her back, but she had the self-awareness to turn her life around. She is still in the transition of it all. She is on her way but not there yet, standing at the credit card terminal with a trembling hand.

Amy

In line behind Lucy stands a woman appearing to be in her early forties who we'll call "Amy." She is very well-dressed and has an aura of confidence and pride while observing the situation around her. As she unloaded items from her cart, she occasionally pauses to make silly faces at the toddler peeking over Lucy's shoulder.

Amy places a value-sized package of organic chicken breasts and a surplus of fresh fruit and veggies onto the conveyor belt, which indicated she understood the importance of incorporating healthy, enriching foods into her and her family's diet. I was made well aware of her commitment to control her children's food portions and her focus on time management by the divided lunch containers she tossed up next. Being in control of your schedule and food intake is vital to success when living a busy life. Although it takes longer to cook these foods versus the microwavable processed alternatives, she budgeted her time and money wisely to provide a healthier lifestyle for her family.

The last thing she unloads is two $30 bottles of red wine, showing she also knows it's acceptable to occasionally and moderately indulge in things she enjoys.

Financially, Amy has reached a place in her life where she can choose the more expensive red wine over a tub of Ben & Jerry's ice cream to fulfill her indulgences. A successful architect, she grew up in a very structured household with parents who advocated for strong and successful habits that would later open up numerous avenues for her success. Her father was a prominent architect in the area and worked to guide her in the direction of an architecture degree. In Amy's case, she had plotted out her timeline and did what was necessary to press on. She prioritized her studies and career over fun or menial relationships because she recognized her potential and took every precaution not to squander it.

Amy gracefully worked her way through her undergrad degree and then tackled her upper grad coursework. Upon receiving her master's degree in architecture, she accepted an internship with a large architectural company and landed a mid-level position at her father's architectural firm. She used this time to learn the ropes and understand some of the "whys" behind her father's executive decisions.

These are the decisions that they don't teach in school and are learned through fieldwork and experience and are exactly what elevates a person from good to great in their respective field. Over time, Amy worked her way up the ranks to an executive position and reached her ultimate goal! She didn't simply jump from one silver spoon-fed opportunity to the next to achieve this goal. When plotting her final goal, she noted smaller checkpoints that would keep her on track to achieve her overall objective.

Life is full of seasons where we plan, hone in on our skills, and execute our goals. This allows us to create incremental accomplishments that ultimately bring us to our overall goal. These incremental goals are important in seeing the progress you've made over time. Each incremental goal is a season in the "sport" of planning, and each of these seasons has a purpose. In-season is where we execute our goals. This is what we have been working for all along, but this really only makes up about 10-25% of our time. This is what you would consider your spotlight or your grand stage.

Now, let's look at the rest of this timeframe. There is an offseason, which is where we'll spend the bulk of our time. Throughout the offseason, we sharpen all of our attributes to prepare us for the following season. The amount of time spent during the offseason is why so many people get discouraged. It's a grueling season that expends a lot of energy. It requires sacrifice. Do you have what it takes to go through the physical and mental preparation to achieve your goals?

This is the time when what you add to your shopping cart matters most. What decisions do you need to make in your preparation to make you stronger?

Once we put in all of the necessary work to ensure our success in the offseason, we fine-tune our skills in the preseason. This is the time just preceding the season when we make sure all of our ducks are in a row with no kinks in the chain. When the preseason is completed, it allows us to enter in-season mentally prepared, and we are able to accept the challenge with great confidence. Then our overall goal is met, and we are positioned as the champions.

The immediate postseason is a time to celebrate your achievements and reflect. This is the shortest of all seasons throughout our timeline. Our celebration is brief yet deserving. As I tell my children, "Act like you've been here before." Achieve success with dignity. In our reflection of the season, we strive to avoid contentment. This is our time to shine, but remember, **flowers don't bloom year-round**. We begin to plot out the timeline leading up to the next season.

> *What attributes could have been stronger leading up to the previous season?*

> *What are our goals for the next season?*

> *What adjustments need to be made to ensure our desired growth?*

This is the season that determines the good and the great. Those who reach a level of success during the in-season and spend the majority of their time in the postseason are those to stall out in a sense of contentment. True, successful entrepreneurs make this the shortest season of all. Their need for gloating is unnecessary and fails to cloud their view of the next mountain. Amy knew how to execute each season accordingly, and this allowed her to be where she is today. She has achieved her goal and is now setting new goals for next season.

In an expansion of the firm, Amy met a newly-introduced executive of equal status. After working closely for some time, they eventually married and began their family. Amy knew what she wanted, executed her plan, and had now cashed in on her hard work. Some will say, "Oh, everything was given to her."

How is that so? What about John? He had a free ride but chose to throw it away. Amy decided to play her winning hand boldly and respectfully. To look at Amy and instantly assume she succeeded due to a silver spoon is not productive, and this way of thinking will be exhibited next in our shopping cart line.

Coming back to the checkout line, Amy has just finished unloading her cart onto the conveyor belt and hears the sound of Lucy's credit card being declined. Lucy shamefully buries her face in her hand. Without hesitation, Amy consoles Lucy, assuring her that everything will be fine before proceeding to pay for Lucy's groceries. At a loss for words and unsure of how to show her gratitude, Lucy hugs her Saving

Grace.

Mike

Last in our line of shoppers, looking in on the scene in front of him, is Mike. He stands in a dingy Metallica t-shirt, slumped over the handle of his cart, sneering at the situation. Mike is an unkempt and clearly unfit individual with an overbearing stench of cheap whiskey and cigarettes.

His cart is piled with a disarray of bad decisions. You can tell his objective when entering the store was to buy two cases of cheap beer and several two liters of soda he clearly planned to use as mixers. This lined the bottom of the cart, and on top of that pile of regret was a mixture of boxed, processed, and frozen foods—frozen pizzas and sugary cereals were tossed rather sloppily next to bags of chips and a loaf of plain white bread.

As he stood behind Amy and Lucy, envying their new friendship, he couldn't help but occasionally glance at the cigarettes behind the counter. There are two possible reasons for the items he chose. The first is that he was so genetically gifted that his nutritional decisions didn't affect his six-pack abs or his optimal overall health. The second was that he shopped out of laziness and convenience, and allowing the wrong items to dictate his budget.

A great visual representation of what is going on in Mike's basket is the "Big rocks of life" demonstration made popular by Stephen Covey in his book *The 7 Habits of Highly Effective People*. In this demonstration, you start with an empty jar. The goal is to fill the jar to the top with no air space remaining. The pillars of your life, "The big rocks," should go into the jar first, as many as would fit.

Then the question is asked, "Is the jar full?" The audience typically answers "Yes."

The next step is to take a number of smaller rocks and drop them into the jar as they will fall within the crevices of the bigger rocks, filling up more space. Again, the question is asked, "Is the jar full?" Everyone again answers, "Yes, surely the jar is full now."

At this point, fine-grain sand is trickled into the jar to fill up even more space. *The jar is definitely full now*, thinks the audience. Lastly, water is poured into the jar and finally fills the jar's air space. This, on a grander scale, is a representation of how Mike failed to create sturdy and productive pillars within his shopping cart. Instead, his pillars were structured on poor habits and the excuse of convenience.

These habits, or guilty pleasures, may carry you through temporarily but can only withstand so much of life's weight before giving out and crumbling down. Guilty pleasures create just that, **guilt**. Do not put guilt and regret into your shopping cart because you absolutely cannot build success on unstable pillars. The fact is, almost all poor decisions are learned behavior that started from somewhere in the timeline of Mike's (and everyone else's) life.

Mike grew up in a lower-middle-class family with an alcoholic father in a home filled with anger, fear, and negativity. As a young child, he had aspirations of being a firefighter, but his dedication to fulfilling that dream faded as he grew up. He was never popular or athletic throughout his childhood, and by middle school was running with a rougher crowd.

In high school, you would almost always find Mike huddled under a cloud of smoke with his friends, camped out behind the football field. Like John, his social life began to impair his decision-making abilities, and he did not pursue his dream of college.

The difference between John and Mike was that John was set up with numerous opportunities to be successful and threw it away. Mike, on the other hand, was given a poor example of what a successful individual or family is supposed to look like. It was up to him to make the necessary changes to break the cycle, yet he continually evaded any responsibility to allow himself to do so. Typically, the apple doesn't fall far from the tree, but every once in a while, a slope at the bottom of the tree enables a particular apple to roll further away.

It is always up to the individual to find this slope and make the decision to get away from the tree that sets them up for failure. However, as Mike moved into his twenties and even thirties, he never changed course. Immediately out of high school, he settled into a factory job with little to no room for growth and dreaded getting up and going to work every day. But it was all that he *felt* he knew how to do. His body was continuously broken down due to the hard labor, and he was unable to recover due to his poor nutritional choices.

Even though the hamster wheel left him miserable, exhausted, and feeling defeated, he chose to stick with the familiar and didn't venture from that path. Mike experienced zero growth and often thought, *I cannot wait to get through paying my dues, so I can sit down to a nice meal, in a nice house, with a wonderful partner and live a wonderful life.* The reality was he didn't have a goal in place to make that happen. He wasn't "paying his dues" at all.

People in Mike's situation are simply living the life that they've chosen for themselves. Think of it as paying rent versus paying a mortgage. Mike was simply paying rent on his life while gaining no equity toward his dreams. Until this perspective is changed, the rent payments are thrown away.

Mike never gained traction because he was never shown the way. He was given poor examples by his parents of what a successful person may look like and was left to navigate on his own. This is why Mike is in the position that he is today. The abundance of bad decisions we make equates to having a daily drink, then deciding to make it a double, and before you know it, you're living in a perpetual hangover. You're exhausted, and you're carrying around an unnecessary load that pulls you down. This can be almost immediately reduced by making better decisions.

The Choice to Be Successful

Here I've shown you four people with four different outlooks, four different journeys, and four vastly different mentalities. John had a good hand and played it poorly. He was once at the top but lost sight of his goals, dragging himself to the bottom. Once in a hole, he made every effort to dig himself out. He experienced both sides of the coin, having luxuries and going without. After experiencing the latter, he knew where he needed to get back to.

Lucy was the product of a few life-altering decisions that did not go her way. Some of these decisions were facilitated by outside sources, but nonetheless, all were choices she made. Through all of her trials and tribulations, Lucy never lost sight of her goal and never lost faith in what was in store for the next chapter of her life.

Amy was dealt an exceptionally good hand, but unlike John, chose to play it well. She had a great support system in place, surrounded herself with positive influences, and never lost sight of the target. She was very strategic in the achievement of each incremental goal to ultimately reach her highest potential. Once that objective was met, she reevaluated where she wanted to go and chose a new objective. Wash, rinse, repeat.

Mike was born into an unmotivated, bad habit-driven life of relative poverty but made little to no effort to remove himself from that life.

On the surface, he was content with the comfort that came with the convenience. But underneath, he felt the constant crushing weight of envy toward those around him who were successful, even though he'd never made an attempt to understand how to achieve it for himself.

The fact is, most people who are unsuccessful make the decision to be unsuccessful, either consciously or unconsciously. They either don't have the drive to get to the next level, they are unable to see the opportunities as they are presented, or they simply can't get out of their own way. Pessimism is typically in the driver's seat and is the truest enabler of failure.

One day I was having a conversation with a patient about different jobs. As she lay there on my treatment table, she made the comment, "Every job sucks. Some people just make more money."

False! I love what I do because I love helping people. Whether it's through chiropractic, motivation, business development, or just a spot at the gym, I love to help people. If you go to work each day and are miserable, then it isn't the job that you hate; it's the decisions that you made to put your life in a position of misery. If you change your way of thinking and the standard in which you gauge your success or happiness, then you'll gain a whole new perspective on your life and the direction it needs to go.

In Robert T. Kiyosaki's *Rich Dad Poor Dad,* he explains being caught in a rat race. The rat race is getting up in the morning to go work for someone else's dream rather than your own. It's the 9-5 cubicle that puts the blinders on your dream and your true, untapped potential. This is how I imagine my patient feels about her situation. Why would you choose to be stuck in a job that you hate? Day in and day out you tediously peck away at a keyboard or you tirelessly slide inanimate objects down a conveyor belt. But why? It's essentially pecking away at the calendar to your financial freedom or watching your dreams convey by one by one.

Our decisions should not only be made for immediate direction but to pave the way for future decisions. For the better part of my twenties, I was a bartender spending night after night pouring drinks at a small town hole-in-the-wall for a bunch of small-time people. It was the type of place where you knew what time it was by who was walking in the door. The same people came in every night at the same time, sat in the same seats, drank the same thing, and had the same mundane conversations. They often complained about how their lives were unsatisfactory and, in turn, took it out on the bar staff.

After becoming fed up with the town, its people, and the lifestyle, I moved to Kansas City on a whim to advance in my personal training career. I didn't know anyone there, but I had to relocate to prevent myself from stalling my success. I didn't want to be a mirror image of those rude, mediocre assholes sitting on the other side of the bar. So I went online and browsed areas with the highest income per capita and decided that's where I wanted to go. As a personal trainer, I needed people with disposable income and was strategic about my move. I interviewed with two gyms in the area and landed a job with a privately-owned gym in one of the richest zip codes in the Midwest, Johnson County, Kansas.

The owner let me stay with his family for a few months until I built up my clientele and got on my feet. I was still working in that small town for the first half of the week, then commuting to Kansas City and offering personal training there the second half. It took a few months, but I was finally able to make the jump and move to Kansas City full-time. I still had some good friends back in that small town, and invited them to come to KC to visit because there were more things to do and mostly because I didn't want to fall back into the trap of that little town. We all know of a person or a place that's a black hole, and to me, that small town was a black hole. I did everything in my power to not get sucked back in.

Five or six years later, I went back to visit a good friend and ended up at that same bar where I had worked. I walked in to find the same people still sitting in their same spots, drinking their same drinks and having their same unbearable conversations. Nothing had changed—not in that bar or in their lives. They were completely content with being mediocre and unsuccessful. Every decision they made up to this point put them in the position of warming that bar stool instead of advancing in life.

I took a minute to evaluate all the growth I had accumulated over the past few years and mentally patted myself on the back for having the courage to remove myself from that toxic environment. Every decision we make, particularly as business owners, must be made with confidence and professionalism, not emotions. That's why I chose to progress through my career the way I did.

I realized that my personal training career would provide a great foundation for my chiropractic career, and it was time to make the transition. Humans are very visually stimulated beings, and maintaining a physically appealing physique at fifty or sixty years old was more than I wanted to put in to attract the amount of clientele I would need to live comfortably. The same goes for chiropractic. There is a window where I have to make a living and invest properly in order to close that chapter and move on. Physically, my body will only be able to take so much.

It was at that time that I had to make yet another decision to be successful. I had to steer my life into a new direction that would allow me to prosper well into my later years. I mentioned earlier that I decided to pursue my doctorate in chiropractic, but what I didn't mention was I did so after swearing I'd never go back to school! However, it aligned well with my personal training background and provided much more structure for success. What I didn't realize (we'll get into the details later) were the opportunities that it would present and just how successful it would allow me to be. I knew changes had to be made, and I made them.

What's Holding You Back?

What is it that keeps us from making the decisions that can change the course of our lives and keep us moving in a positive direction? Are we simply afraid that we cannot withstand the humility that comes with failure? Are we confused about the direction in which we should point our life's compass? How do we know which direction is correct? In short, we don't. We have to trust our instincts and our previous experiences to tell us that this is the direction we should be traveling. **You have to remember that our hindsight of one failure is our foresight of the next successful endeavor.** Before all else, you have to make the decision to just begin.

Our decisions do not rest on the shoulders of others. They are a part of us, ingrained in our beings, longing to express themselves with an amplified impact on the world. Other groups or individuals may influence the direction that you choose to steer your heading, but it is your choice nonetheless. You must choose to act in a way that aligns your decisions with the direction that you want your life to go. Life is a competition. Regardless of what anyone says, you're competing against others for professional rank, for social status, for economic gains—there's always something! You're also competing against yourself, striving to be a better version of yourself. If you're not competing with yourself, then I don't expect you to be reading this book.

Externally, we are competing with the masses, but internally it is only you versus you. Competition is a healthy way of life and feeds your drive. If you're reading this book, then you're eager to excel because you want to do better; you want to be better. People who constantly complain about their status yet exhibit poor work ethics and lack the drive to succeed will remain exactly where they are. They will continue spinning their wheels on the low end of the totem pole and looking up at the top without a clue of how to get there. People who are constantly worried about the status of another will also trudge slowly. I am not contradicting my previous statement of competing with others for status. You simply cannot "worry" about what the other person is doing to get there. Worrying is an emotion that will deplete you of optimism. They have their own journey. Work on you!

Notice, I say "work" on you, not "worry" about you. If you're worried about yourself, then you're afraid of failure or afraid of making good judgments. Make the decisions that will make you the most successful. My favorite chart that I frequently reference shows the different habits between successful and unsuccessful people. Among other differences, it states that successful people will talk about ideas, whereas unsuccessful people will talk about other people.

Successful people will fulfill their lives with positivity and knowledge, and they are never too arrogant to admit there is always more to learn. Do not waste your efforts or your time on the parts of life that are out of your control. Put the correct items in your shopping cart, and your life will begin to blossom. Remember, you're the only one responsible for what gets added to your cart.

CHAPTER 3
THE DOPAMINE RESPONSE

Between stimulus and response there is a space.
In that space is our power to choose our response.
In our response lies our growth and our freedom.
~ Viktor E. Frankl

Have you ever driven down the highway and spotted something off in the distance, and all of a sudden, you notice your vehicle begins to steer slowly in that direction? It's generally followed by a quick jerk, a hard correction back onto the highway, and a big sigh of relief. The objective in life is to keep it between the lines. This is our productive space. Our goals in life rest at the end of this metaphorical highway, however, along the side are the distractions and temptations that want to deter us from those goals. This causes us to veer off into the rocky terrain that leads us down unproductive and/or self-destructive paths.

These diversions are called dopamine responses—habits that form in our everyday lives that, for better or worse, seem to affect how we live. We grow accustomed to the habits we form and seldom stray with little variance because we are creatures of habit. My wife and I have eight children. Oh yeah, you read that right—eight children! That means eight mouths to feed, eight extracurricular schedules to manage, and eight personalities to keep on the straight and narrow. Over the course of our relationship, we've done our best to manage any behavioral issues. In order to do that, I had to think of a way to create visuals that would help them stay on track. I drew up a road analogy with my children to help set boundaries in their lives and provide some guidance to bolster their resistance to making emotional or impulsive decisions. I used the road to demonstrate standing firm in our boundaries by staying within the lines. At the top of the road, I had each child write their goals along with an expectation that we may have for them. I left the shoulders of the highway blank for them to list what could be some temptations that they currently struggle with.

When I asked my kids to give me some examples they could write on the road to help keep them going in a positive direction, they responded with things like "being respectful," "staying organized," and "listening." When asked to list actions that might cause us to get off track, they listed things like "interrupting," "bullying," and "inappropriate words or content." These are all standards they set for themselves within the parameters of their age groups and maturity levels. However, the goals that we set for ourselves are merely checkpoints, and the road continues on with new goals, different temptations, and more severe consequences.

Now that we know our entire life hinges on the decisions that we make, it's pertinent to know how those decisions are made and how they ultimately determine which direction those hinges allow your door to swing. By doing this, I was able to make them aware of the parameters in which they need to abide in order to avoid "crashing." This is a lesson that can be referred to regarding childhood, adulthood, business, relationships, life, and so on. There will always be temptations that rest in the distance, luring you to steer away from your goals, which is why it's necessary to have an elevated amount of discipline to keep your "vehicle" controlled through each checkpoint.

Each time you encounter an exciting and/or engaging experience, your body produces a hormone called dopamine, a neurotransmitter that helps control the areas in the brain that identify with reward and pleasure. As we begin to taste this "drug," so to speak, our bodies lose responsiveness to it, and we seek out an increased amount of dopamine-releasing behaviors to recreate that initial "high."

Jeremy Dean states in his book *Making Habits, Breaking Habits*, "Activities we once considered painful, like getting up early to go to work, become less so with repetition. On the other hand, activities that excite us or bring us pleasure initially, like sex, beer or listening to Beethoven's 7th, soon become mundane. Of course, we fight against the leaking away of pleasure, sometimes with success, by seeking variety. This is why some people feel they have to keep pushing the boundaries of experience to get the same high."

Creating your high with a productive source will inevitably push you to want to recreate it through positive and healthy habits. On the contrary, an initial high through a negative stimulus will undoubtedly send you in the other direction. That is something that you have to keep under control. Otherwise, your entire life, business or anything else will implode. As we excessively allow impulsive actions, we create this underlying feeling of "waiting for the other shoe to drop." On the outside, these immediately gratifying decisions promote a sense of fulfillment, but trapped within ourselves, we feel an overwhelming burden that shifts our focus to negative stimuli that only strays us further from our goals.

This feeling that consumes you only brings your attention to the fact that you could implode at any moment, forcing you to rebuild and start again. These individuals are often labeled as "risk takers." While risk-taking is a trait directly related to the success of an entrepreneur, risks absolutely must be calculated. Failure to do so will create an opening that will surely lead you down the wrong path.

Why do "dopamine junkies" crave this stimulation? The need for constant stimulation may be due to an individual not receiving adequate stimulation as a child or being overly stimulated as a child and having that stimulation taken away in adulthood. It's possible that an individual is genetically susceptible to acquiring this trait of seeking out risk-taking behaviors. Regardless of the reason, it is up to us to decipher which risks are calculated and which are naive, fueled by our dopamine cravings.

The negative stimulus that surrounds us daily will breed insecurity and a false sense of reality if we let it. Remember John from *The Shopping Cart?* When John was no longer being stimulated and rewarded positively by football, he began seeking out negative stimuli to fill the void created by an otherwise unstable and unfulfilled life. Our society has become a predator to these individuals, constantly demanding engagement, and it becomes almost impossible to shut it off once it's been turned on. Dopamine-driven decisions that begin to seem almost autonomic can endanger our ability to continuously drive towards success.

We must harness our thoughts and actions to aim them at the productive bullseye. As our brain begins to develop more of these nonproductive, autonomic thoughts, we, unfortunately, become a dismantling robot, tearing away at the advancements we've made toward our goal. Self-control is essential when reining in these compulsive needs for impulsivity.

If you somehow haven't noticed, there are stimuli all around us—television commercials, internet ads, the titles of every Facebook ad, video games, etc. These are just a few mediums that have strategically placed dopamine-attracting features that trigger the addictive response in your body on an everyday basis. The *New York Post* released a study stating that Americans check their phone, on average, 80 times per day, and that isn't even considering the many other mediums of dopamine-releasing stimuli we are exposed to.

Just because the little notification on your phone is telling you that you have a text, Facebook notification, a Snapchat, or whatever else, doesn't mean that you must check it or give your time and energy to it. It will still be there when you check it five minutes from now, an hour later, or tomorrow. I know it's easier said than done because as I'm typing this, I just instinctively picked up my phone when it dinged. It is anywhere and everywhere.

How do your actions resonate with the little red notification of your subconscious mind? Better yet, what are your reactions? Are you impulsively acting on every little "ding" that occurs in your mind? Are you capable of fulfilling your daily obligations without the need to clear the red notification from your screen? The majority of these tasks, if you can even call some of them a task, will be there when you're ready to open them, without penalty, without distraction, and without the sense of culpability.

Pertaining to business, why not turn the tables? I just said that these stimuli feed on us, so make it work for you. If you're an entrepreneur, which you are if you chose to open this book, then utilize this method to attract people to your product. Make your brand so irresistible that the consumer cannot resist. Have you ever seen an Instagram account that cranks out the same material you're providing, yet they get to ten times the viewers? It's a science! Algorithms, timing, keywords, and presentation are all intricate parts that turn brands into money-making machines.

There is no reason why you can't capture the same audience and drive that traffic to your own product. So, what are you missing in your brand that is stopping you from being an addicting and priceless commodity? We'll get into more of the "how," but for now, I'll keep things simple: be the addiction; don't be the addicted!

It is rare that individuals just fall into the right place at the right time and experience continued success. Successful people not only put themselves in the right place at the right time, they pay attention to what is going on around them at all times. They are not consumed with fulfilling their impulsive needs; rather, they are mindful of the potential opportunities at their fingertips. They are engaged listeners, attentive and mindful of any potentially beneficial information that may come their way.

Our personal and professional relationships diminish as we often try to recreate the surreal lives of our "friends" and colleagues that we see through endless and meaningless dopamine responses until we become emotionally depleted. At this point, we are unable to utilize clear judgment and begin making irrational decisions to fulfill instant gratification. Theodore Roosevelt said, "Comparison is the thief of joy." You cannot compare yourself to others and end up successful. With social media being a crucial part of the new age entrepreneur, we must seek to empower our formidable presence while simultaneously being impervious to negative stimuli.

During a meeting with my friend and social media advisor, I expressed my frustration with the lack of engagement that I was receiving on social media compared to others on my timeline. I was wasting my time and energy with these comparative feelings. It's not that I even compared material items or luxuries that others had in their posts. I had just grown frustrated by worthless posts receiving thousands of likes while I would provide great quality content and get maybe fifty likes.

I couldn't understand what I was doing wrong. I often asked myself, *Are these people better than me?* I had to remind myself that I was only getting beat by bullshit, bots, and algorithms.

Seeking Out the Positive

We've already covered that our world is a very stimulating place. You're the only one who can determine where you get stimulation. Only you can choose whether you're affected by positive or negative stimuli. Positive stimuli stem from production and advancement towards a plotted, well-thought-out goal. Most businesses are initially created from only a business plan. Within a business plan, financial projections are produced to plot out incremental goals. Monthly, quarterly, yearly, and three to five-year goals are set. As these milestones are achieved, a positive stimulus helps to satisfy the need to seek out any behaviors resulting in a negative dopamine response.

Not only does this provide you the gratification of your achievement, but it creates a template of how to achieve future goals faster and more efficiently and allows for more frequent positive stimuli to occur. Imagine for a moment a number line with integers traveling in either direction. You have positive and negative integers, just like you have positive and negative stimuli. We all start at zero and, one way or another, are pushed in a certain direction. The more positive behaviors that you implement into your life, the further you get down the positive side of the number line, and the opposite will occur through negative behaviors.

I was discussing macroeconomics and the impulsiveness of consumer decision-making with a friend who's a graduate student of economics at Texas A&M. In a nutshell, he explained the concept as an individual's ability to make a rational decision directly relies on that individual's ability to utilize all possible means to arrive at the most educated decision. The further we deviate from this line of rationality with decisions that are based on behavioral needs, the greater the dopamine response will be in our lives. Look at my wife and me. I like to think of us as The Detail Chick and the Idea Guy, which has inspired our blog and other projects.

She keeps me steered straight because, well, I'm fucking impulsive. However, my ideas are also explosive! Her ability to harness all of that explosive energy and apply the incremental steps necessary is what makes the engine run. We'll talk about the importance of placing people in your life who will best complement your strengths and accommodate your weaknesses during the chapter *Your Inner Circle*.

Oftentimes, our impulsive behaviors cause us to overload ourselves, ultimately preventing any new growth. Maybe it's not biting off more than we can chew but rather piling too much on our plate to begin with. I can still hear my mom saying, "I think your eyes are bigger than your stomach." I am constantly having new ideas floating around in my head and find myself unable to shut my brain off most of the time. I've mentioned the benefit of a business plan in any new endeavor, but it's important to note, this is something that you should do with your life goals as well.

Recently, my wife and I have been discussing a number of investment opportunities that we want to accomplish and had the ideas spread out across the board. If you recall from Chapter 1, our Workshop Wednesdays are instrumental as brainstorming sessions, where we bounce ideas and do deeper dives into promising opportunities. Some of our ideas have come and gone, others have merged, some have evolved, and some stand strong. We made an investment timeline for ourselves, plotting many of those previous ideas into precise objectives. Our initial timeline had random dates on when we thought we would be able to achieve that particular task. The completion of this book sat as one of the very first objectives to complete, although it has proven to be one of my most difficult.

After the timeline was put together, we began to go over the financial aspects of the obstacles we had plotted out. The order or completion times of a few ideas just didn't make sense. We then sat down to revise our timeline by putting them in the order of which investments could lead to the next by creating a snowball effect. Each investment rolls into the next, providing capital for the following investment, growing our finances and the size of each investment. There is a difference between being productive and being impulsive. Productivity is acting assertively on a well-thought-out plan to achieve a specific task, while impulsivity is jumping the gun, in turn making you more vulnerable to mistakes.

Since every idea was, at the time, a "good idea," we didn't jump into anything that would set us back in the long run. Although initial ideas may be good ideas, forcing them into existence with poor timing and impulsivity can fuck up your whole world. Just as good investments can allow you to grow, poor investments can cause a snowball effect too, but in a negative manner. Imagine yourself pushing a snowball up a hill, and that snowball represents hard-earned income from assertive and well-calculated moves. It takes more work and more time to grow in size.

Now imagine on the other side, a snowball rolling down the hill. This snowball represents poorly calculated decisions and rapidly increasing debt. One major slip and you'll lose control of the snowball, causing it to rapidly pick up steam and increase in size at a tremendous pace. I've heard too many horror stories about entrepreneurs who jump on the bandwagon of a new idea by using the financial resources of an existing endeavor. One miscalculation can turn a potentially good investment into a poor investment, draining not only the financial resources set aside for the endeavor but also the money stream that you're using to funnel into the project.

Blackjack

Imagine, for a moment, that two men are sitting at a blackjack table. The first man is sitting comfortably with millions of dollars in his bank account, and the second man is desperate to win a big score with only a thousand dollars in his bank account. Both men place their bets of a thousand dollars. The dealer has a five showing, and if you aren't an experienced blackjack player, this is the highest probability bust card. Both gentlemen have two face cards each, giving them both twenty. The first man, contently sitting in his seat, calmly waves off any more cards while the second man is anxiously bouncing in his seat, eager to see the dealer bust so he can double his money and head back home (or perhaps seek out further dopamine in the slot machines across the casino). He, too, waves off any more cards.

The dealer flips over a six of hearts, making eleven. Obligated to hit, the dealer takes another card, and it's a face card. The dealer hits 21 and rakes in both men's chips. The second man throws his head into his hands in utter disbelief. He lost all of his money in a desperate attempt to win big. The first man, still calm, antes up for the next hand without hesitation. The moral of the story? While both men bet the same amount of money, the second man was impulsive, betting out of desperation, whereas the first man had calculated his risks and was basically unaffected by his loss. Know your strategy beforehand and stick to it. Venturing from a well-thought-out plan will only lead to a decline in performance and success. For me, I always have my limits, I only play what I can afford to lose, and I never hit 16. Beyond those rules, I play the game aggressively, just as I do in all other areas of my life.

Here's the caveat. Our ability to know when to "hit" and when to "stay" is directly related to decision-making in our everyday lives. How are you responding to temptations at life's blackjack table? Are you letting your hasty decisions dictate how you live your life? Are you unable to see past your own impulsive, self-sabotaging decisions to know that that is what is keeping you from moving forward with your life? These are the kinds of questions that you must start asking yourself before you start getting any sort of answers to your struggles.

Impulsive decisions can be the death of your business and become a burden on your everyday life, and it ties into *The Shopping Cart* chapter.

Just recently, I was meeting a friend at a local Starbucks to discuss some money management changes that she could make to assist in some financial progress. She mentioned that it seemed no matter how much she made or what she did, she still felt like she was barely scraping by at the end of each pay period. So, we set up a meeting to review her budget.

As a consultant, I am very straightforward, and there is never any sugarcoating. You have to be able to acknowledge the issues and make the necessary changes to see any change. As I was pulling in a few minutes early to set up, I sent her a text that said, "Hey, I am pulling in now. What would you like? I can go ahead and grab it." She replied, "I am on my way. Don't worry about my drink. I placed an online order for a latte."

What?! She is unable to maintain a budget but is somehow capable of impulsively and possibly routinely ordering a $5 coffee? Why she would do this made no sense to me, but it was then apparent exactly why she was fighting this biweekly battle of keeping money in the bank. As we sat down to begin, she looked at me over her cup with a euphoric eye roll like she was drinking crack.

"I needed this," she said.

"No," I replied. "You convinced yourself you needed that. You needed that $5 to stay in your account. The reason that you're unable to maintain any kind of balance in your account is not because you aren't making enough money or your fixed monthly overhead is too high. It's your spending habits."

It was apparent that was not what she wanted to hear, having some cold, hard truth splashed into her hot, steamy $5 latte. Impulsive decisions will fill your shopping cart with needless "stuff." Don't be the broke woman carrying around a Louis Vuitton bag with a fresh set of nails just to appear like you're of a status you aren't. Financial freedom comes with time. Her impulsive decision to buy that latte gives instant gratification but long-term disappointment.

She expressed that she works hard and pays her bills but doesn't want to give up the few things that she enjoys. I promise you, financial stability is much more enjoyable. We sat for the next half hour talking about some modifications that she could make to avoid the paycheck-to-paycheck struggle. Some of the hindrance items she identified were out of impulsive cravings and convenience, while some were out of pure laziness. We scheduled a follow-up meeting for a month out. In our next meeting, it was very obvious, just from her prideful mannerisms, that she had been successful in resisting splurging and impulsive buys. She admitted she did not eliminate them from her life completely yet had reduced them dramatically. She recognized that her level of stability improved and allowed her to grow her account and relieve some of her stress.

I can be this honest in these situations because I've been there. I'm living proof that you can hit the bottom and turn it around into a success story. My early twenties were nothing short of rockstar status. All I was missing was the rockstar income. I didn't have a care in the world, except for my oldest son, Jacob, who was born when I was only 22 years old. He lived two hours away with his mother, so outside of my designated times with him, I was living it up. Responsibilities and priorities meant nothing to me. I knew that if I fell, there would be someone there to pick me up, saying it was okay and enabling the continual, same destructive behavior.

I always maintained a safety net. I was working in the previously mentioned small bar at the time and lived in an apartment above another restaurant that my boss owned. His owning the restaurant and apartment was both a safety net and a burden. It was a safety net because I knew he would never kick me out. However, I had to see him every day at work.

At this time in my life, not only was I living paycheck to paycheck, but was carelessly living from one party to the next. I reveled in life with one impulsive behavior after another, digging myself into a hole that took me a decade to crawl out of. It was the lowest of my lows.

One particular Friday afternoon, during a snowy winter, I drove an hour to pick up my oldest son, who was three years old at the time. After driving another hour back, I returned to a dark, freezing cold apartment. I flipped on the light switch, and luckily the lights came on. Our gas, however, which powered my heat, had been shut off. Jacob and I both put on a few layers of clothes and cuddled up under a mound of blankets in the bed. The wind howled outside as it blew in a fresh white blanket of snow, and our covers became no match for the dropping temperatures.

I then remembered that my oven was electric, so I told Jacob to keep covered in the bed until I came back to get him. I went into the kitchen, turned the oven on, and opened the door to heat the kitchen. I quickly hurried back into the bedroom, grabbed the pillows, all the blankets, and my shivering child, and made us a pallet on the kitchen floor. We were able to make our way through the night and call to get someone out the next day to get the gas turned back on. All I could think about as we lay huddled up on the kitchen floor in front of that open oven was, *My choices caused this.*

It goes back to our decisions directly reflecting our place in life. My impulsive decisions put my son and me in a bad and potentially dangerous situation. It wasn't only the present time that my son was affected. Sure, he was cold at that moment, but it serves as a reminder that we don't have to be unnecessarily cold if we make the right decisions. Right then, I made the decision to never end up here again. I had to start intentionally living with more integrity and focus on bettering the life of not only myself but my child.

It wasn't soon after that I decided to finish school and get away from that lifestyle as I recognized the steady decline and that my life was at an all-time low. There is one thing about these low points, though. Hitting them will make you hungry for something better. Your lowest low can inspire your highest high if you let it.

Don't Put It Off

Have you ever had that friend or colleague, or maybe even yourself, who starts a project and completes a substantial amount of the work just to stop and leave it incomplete? This is not my normal modus operandi, or "MO." However, in one instance, I got stuck in procrastination purgatory. For some reason, writing this book became a seemingly never-ending challenge. I'd been working on it for quite some time when Ford Taylor, a strategist, public speaker, and published author came into my office. We began discussing the contents of my manuscript and various topics, including entrepreneurial topics in general. At the end of each appointment, he asked, "Have you finished your book yet?"

After a few months of routine appointments, I repeatedly answered "no" to his question. Then I began dodging the question. *If I just keep talking, he won't have a chance to get it out,* I told myself. However, he found a way to get it in there. I told him that I was so busy in the office that by the end of the day, I had no creative juices left to pen quality content. I was frustrated at being so close to the end yet so far away from completing what I had set out to accomplish.

Again, it was uncharacteristic of me to procrastinate, but at this point, I'd been sitting around 75% finished for months with no real sprint to the finish. Close to 20 pages needed to be strategically inserted to achieve my desired word count. I had to edit, publish, create awareness, find an agent, and market the hell out of it to make sales. There were a lot of steps that I continually pushed off or put on the "book back burner," always defaulting to the needs of my office and the time commitments of my family life.

One afternoon, Ford came in for another routine visit, and after our normal interaction proceeded to tell me a story of Dan, a guy he worked with in a small group. Dan was notorious for starting projects and walking away before they were complete. When Ford picked up on this nonproductive habit, he decided to take action. One day, he and Dan were sitting in their small group when Ford called him out. He told the group, "Okay, from now on, we'll call Dan the '75% guy' until he no longer leaves things unfinished. Once he improves, he can be Dan again." Damn, harsh, bro!

We went through the remainder of Ford's appointment, and I walked him to the front desk receptionist to get him rescheduled. I stood there as he made an appointment and paid. As he started walking towards the door, I said, "Bye, Mr. Taylor."

"See ya later, 75% guy," he replied as he smiled and exited the office.

He straight-up called me out on my procrastination. He knew from the extent of our conversations that I had so far produced quality content for the book, but unless it was finished and released to the public, the effort would be deemed worthless. From then on, each time Mr. Taylor arrived at the office, he smiled and addressed me, once again, as "75% guy." This motivated me to press forward and complete the book. At that point, I got to be Dr. Allen again.

So many distractions can pull us away from our goals. Impulsive behaviors, like the addictions of binging shows on Netflix, overwork, daily alcohol or weed urges, pornography, nonproductive texting, or mindless scrolling on social media, can all take away from the time we could be investing elsewhere. The dopamine response strikes again.

Have you ever checked your screen time? It'll surely make you cringe. Newer phones now have an app or setting that not only allows you to check your total amount of time spent on your device but breaks it down into different categories, making you aware of what is productive and nonproductive. Those categories should reflect your business accordingly to maximize not just your time but the value of your time.

Long hours (and a lot of caffeine) of cranking out material, determined to not be the 75% guy.

The Impulse vs. Procrastination Conundrum

Here's the kicker. We cannot be impulsive, and at the same time, we cannot procrastinate. It's problematic unless you know how to thoughtfully consider opportunities and thoughtfully act upon them before they disappear. It's a balancing skill set that successful entrepreneurs have mastered and an example of the business reflexes we develop over time. Until then, we may feel paralyzed because our ability to assess and move quickly is limited. Or, we might make a manic and potentially disastrous move (the dopamine response).

Both procrastination and impulsive behavior will undoubtedly facilitate a sympathetic nervous response. This is our fight-or-flight response. Being in this state for a prolonged period promotes reactionary responses. I think it goes without saying that "reactionary" is interchangeable with "impulsive." The bottom line is we are still hampered by conditioned impulsive behaviors that seem to steal our attention or distract us from rationality. It often causes us to set aside our more goal-oriented or productive tasks.

For instance, there is an art and science to problem-solving, and it involves two main character types—those who are dominant and decisive and those who are analytical. They operate in different ways. I don't claim that one is better than the other because both have pros and cons. However, a dominant person like me generally doesn't procrastinate. I'm able to process an opportunity without wasting time, and simply make decisions, execute those decisions, and then move on to the next item on the horizon.

This is how I tend to operate in business too. I don't sit back and ponder the possibilities of success. I go after it! I calculate my risks and pull the trigger, unlike an analytical person who tends to make sure (or overthink) the ins and outs of the problem. If someone asks the analytical guy about the problem, he better be able to spit out a direct answer rather than hemming and hawing over a ton of data points. If you're going to be analytical, then ask the right questions and learn how to pull the trigger.

In other words, in a precautionary sense, don't be overly analytical. *That,* indeed, was the root of my procrastination in writing this book! I got lost in the weeds. It took a client and his moniker jab—"75% guy"—to kick-start the creative process and nudge me toward the goal.

Think about it. Why second-guess yourself when you can focus on the larger picture and push through? Why question and re-question minutia that will get lost in translation anyway? When I find myself in a progression stalemate, I'm overstimulating myself with the things that don't matter rather than honing in on things that do. Responsibilities and obligations aren't accomplished on autopilot. This, obviously, is an example of living in avoidance and denial, and believe me, never again will I allow myself to sputter out. My next book, already in the works, is on track due to these valuable insights and lessons.

Things do not just "go away." As we'll address in the *Your Perspective is Your Objective* chapter, businesses can default to autopilot too, which can lead to a dramatic crash-and-burn scenario. We have to have the discipline and willpower to overcome avoidance urges and power through whatever "procrastination purgatory" threatens our momentum.

A determining factor that ultimately promotes success is the ability to maintain discipline in all facets of your life. Discipline is a necessary constant as motivation will come and go. Those who require external motivation tend to fall off. The ability to execute through discipline will carry you further than your "motivated" competitor. It's loading our shopping cart with productive habits that streamline our success. It's the decision to pre-make our meals versus going out to eat. It's repelling the sudden urge to stop off at the bar instead of going to the gym on your way home from work. It's the ability to ignore these urges and remain on course.

These are all examples of avoiding dopamine-driven deterrents to keep our lives moving in the right direction. Giving in to impulsive behaviors will result in procrastination from the tasks that are needed for you, your goals, your businesses, or your endeavors to grow. Constantly giving in to the little red notification on your smartphone or the urge to mindlessly scroll social media posts is a negative time-waster. It neglects your growth. Who cares what anyone else is doing? They aren't going to get you closer to your goal.

Do not stagnate productivity with the idea that we need frequent breaks to remain sharp. Do not put off until tomorrow what needs to be done today. No matter what the reason, your goals will not be reached when your life is constantly interrupted by dopamine-infused triggers. Our ideas actually require a shit load of work—not mindless distractions.

Why do gyms that were full in January seem to be empty by February 1st? Why do people drop out of school? Why do people quit smoking only to pick it back up a month later when something stresses them out? They lose focus on their goals and fail to be disciplined and overcome these conditioned urges.

What is that one thing that you just cannot seem to turn off or get rid of? Do you tell yourself, *Okay, I am truly going to eat clean all month this time!* but then you attend a birthday party, and the cake just keeps eyeballing you? Have you told yourself that you aren't going to drink anymore, but when your friends all hold their glasses up for a New Year's Eve toast, you don't want to be the only one drinking water, so you give in and order a cocktail? These are your little red notifications. These are life's ways of deterring us from our projected path. The decision to ignore these distractions is what keeps us moving in the right direction toward innately (naturally) becoming successful.

Newsflash! There will always be things that you don't want to do in business that you'll either have to personally attend to or delegate. The worst thing that you can do is to leave it pending. How many times has impulsiveness caused you to put something on the back burner, resulting in penalties, and then want to kick yourself in the butt because you know better?

Work First, Play Later

While work might tempt us toward procrastination, play is typically impulsive. I teach my kids, *work first, play later*. We "think" we need that dopamine rush, but playing first and working last is a form of procrastination that leads to future anxiety. And worse, it can lead to impulsive decisions in an attempt to make up for the deficit. It's like putting a bandage over a gunshot wound, or as I say in the office, "It's like putting Icy Hot on a torn muscle." It may mask the pain, but it doesn't resolve the problem, and in all reality, just makes the problem worse. Over time, the severity will become too much and the injury will eventually completely tear, rendering you useless.

Take money as another example. We cannot put ourselves in unnecessary financial holes and burn the bridges that can lead us to better places. We cannot fall victim to difficult circumstances. Treat the problem at its core! You do not become a better person by masking the symptoms, and you cannot heal yourself until you diagnose the fact that you have an impulse problem and change your life.

How many of us leave mail on the desk, and before we know it, we have Mount Everest towering over our work day? No one likes being hassled by the burden of bills, but no one likes to be burdened with consequent fines and penalties either. If you have the tendency to overlook important documents that come in the mail, then find your solution. Almost every vendor will allow you to set up an autopay now, so set it up. Automate your life! That is one less thing that you have to worry about, and if you already know that you procrastinate, then why not do it? We have the technology to do almost anything that we want, so why not take advantage of this to become more efficient? Prioritize and think of autodraft as an assistant. Remember those smart decisions mentioned in *The Shopping Cart?* Make those smart choices personally and professionally and maximize your time. Time is the most valuable commodity you can accrue. The time you waste could cost you a huge opportunity.

Your time is only as valuable as you make it. Time is money. If you tell yourself that you're a three or even four-figure-an-hour person, then you will be. If you tell yourself that you're worth minimum wage, then you will, instead, achieve a minimum wage. Don't cut into your time with things that do not matter. Exploit every opportunity to stay ahead and prosper.

The Zone of Optimal Performance

Procrastination has other ramifications. Not only does it take away from your time, but also takes away from your performance. This brings to mind the advice I share with my children as they play sports. I encourage them to have control over their emotions when they are playing. Emotion can cause misjudgment and mistakes. The apple didn't fall far from the tree because I, myself, am insanely competitive and passionate on the field and in the gym. I'm afraid they've all inherited this behavior—or I have failed to fully disconnect from my father's way of parenting, which has caused them to mimic my same behavior.

I tell them a certain level of stimulation is needed to perform at their best. But if they're overly emotional or frustrated, their performance will decline. However, the same is true if they aren't stimulated enough. Achieving an optimal zone of arousal is key. In the early 1900s, the Yerkes-Dodson law (the empirical relationship between pressure and performance) was presented in a bell diagram, showing the relationship between arousal levels and their effects on performance. When a child is blessed with a structured household, this structure will typically follow them into adulthood. They mirror the blueprint that was laid out, making adjustments that accommodate their lives.

On the other hand, a child raised in an unstructured home must be the architect in designing the productive structure from scratch. The more solid we build our foundation, the stronger our decision-making skills will become. Everything will seem to fall into place.

Maintaining a balance between impulsive behaviors and procrastination allows you to stay in your optimal performance zone.

Everyone's zone is different, and the bell curve skews for all. Your "zone" is not someone else's zone. It's not your team's zone, it's not your parent's zone, and it's not your spouse's zone—it's your zone! However, it's not a comfort zone, so let's not make a misinterpretation. This is our zone of optimal performance. To be in this zone, it takes a lot of time learning to be comfortable with the uncomfortable.

What do you need to do to kill it? You cannot conform to someone else's mold. Don't be a lemming, be a leader. Bottom line, the key to avoiding procrastination and impulsivity is productive stimuli! Only you know what that takes. Light that fire under your own ass and get moving! Whether it's loud music when working out, imagery to prepare for a big event, audiobooks for motivation to accomplish your goals, phone reminders to alert you when you need to tackle work tasks, or simply putting things on the calendar and checking them off—get it done.

The more consistent that you remain with "feeding" yourself productive stimuli, the easier it will be to continue an upward trend toward success.

CHAPTER 4
BE ENTICING

Conformity is the jailer of freedom and the enemy of growth
~ John F. Kennedy

When my son, Tyson, began his college football recruiting process towards the end of his junior year, the level of enticement was evident—in a big way. From the moment they stepped foot in the baggage claim, their bags were whisked away to a fleet of black SUVs, surrounded by the entire coaching staff. Each member of our family was given a room full of favorite snacks, drinks, and personalized swag. The potential recruits were taken on elaborate photo and video shoots, to coaches' personal homes, and treated to luxurious dinners, just to name a few. On one particular visit, a black Cadillac SUV made a four-hour drive and pulled up in front of our house to escort Tyson and my wife to the airport, which was eight minutes away. They were flown out and wined and dined for a long weekend and then were sent back to a life of normalcy.

This far surpassed any level of recruiting I encountered as a wrestler. In the south, it's a low-budgeted and overlooked sport compared to the giant shadow that is Texas football. There were no MaxPreps or 247Sports to provide easily accessible rankings and player information to coaches. There was no Hudl platform to upload professional-esque highlight videos, complete with music and animated graphics. Not yet did we have the luxury of Instagram or X (Twitter) to communicate with the preferred college coaching staff or announce to the world that we had just rushed for 237 yards and 4 touchdowns the night before. Hell no! My little teenage ass sat on the floor in my parent's living room with two VCRs, a box full of videos of my wrestling matches, and a handful of blank VHS tapes.

In VCR one, I inserted each of my match tapes one by one and pushed play while simultaneously pressing the record button on VCR two, which had the blank tape. I repeated the process until I recorded enough content to show the college coaches what I was capable of. I then had to put the finished highlight copy into the VCR and watch it dozens of times while recording that onto the other blank tapes, so I had multiple copies.

My dinosaur-era "filmography" landed me a recruiting trip to Missouri Valley College, a smaller NAIA college that seemed to be a good feeder school into some of the bigger Division I schools. Their approach was quite the opposite of what Tyson was offered. Basically, my mother and I were shown around campus, which was practically one square block. I was greeted by a few of the senior wrestlers, separated from my mother, and taken to a small house where they proceeded to feed me alcohol and introduce me to the local college girls. It worked! This was, at the time, the best night of my life. I was living the college life, sitting on cloud nine, and eager to sign on the dotted line as soon as I got back.

Then reality set in. I pulled into the small town of Marshall, Missouri, one August day in 2000 with all of my belongings in tow. When I walked onto campus, I noticed that it was nothing like the recruiting trip. Everyone was back in the routine of the school year, wrestling itself was a job, and the social life reversed into a drab disappointment. I chose my book by its cover, so to speak, and contents weren't really that appealing.

Fast forwarding back from the Stone Age to the present, we have a much more elaborate approach to the recruiting game. It was very important for Tyson's mom and me to explain what the enticement meant. All of the shininess thrown at him was exciting but deserved a closer look—a level-headed dive into reality. No doubt, each college exhibits a tremendous opportunity, but what are you actually getting? Did these campuses offer a catalyst to get him to the next level? Would it help set him up for life overall—life off the football field? To Tyson's credit, he didn't want a business transaction. He wanted a personal and enriching college experience.

We really had to weigh the importance of what each school offered and created a spreadsheet to track and compare areas of importance.

On the list, we noted the academic focus, location of the school, the culture of the team, football ranking, track ranking, future network of the alumni, the quarterback, what position or sport he was being recruited for, the makeup of the other commits, and, finally NIL (name, image, likeness) opportunities. In the preceding story, the school checked most boxes (very highly) but goes to show that certain faults or blemishes can resonate poorly with your consumer. Outside of what the school has to offer, it was very important to us, particularly Tyson, to connect on a more personal level. He did not want to be sold on the bells and whistles of a business transaction. He wanted to know that he was valued and would be pushed to grow as a person.

In my opinion, being attractive or enticing comes from authenticity. When an organization is authentic, it shows. When you are authentic, it shows. When you are not, it blatantly tarnishes the shininess of your brand, your product, and yourself. When you are the consumer on the receiving end of the deal, this aura of superficiality or artificiality will come to the forefront, negating the worth of the item being sold.

I was unable to attend another one of the recruiting visits for Tyson, and my wife, Kathy, traveled with him to observe what the school's program had to offer. Upon getting to the campus, they were showered with gifts and promised a number of perks. After settling into the room and rummaging through the welcome bags left by the recruiting department, they made their way to lunch. Culturing the recruits, it was customary to indulge in a number of the local delicacies. The three of them, Tyson, Kathy, and the head coach stood at the counter, staring up at the menu hanging above the counter. Once they ordered, they stood at the food pick-up window and waited for their orders.

The coach's food was first placed on the ledge of the window. Without hesitation, he grabbed his tray and made his way to the table. Kathy and Tyson continued waiting, and then proceeded to the table, where they found the coach insatiably devouring his meal. Without comment, they sat down and dined while conversing with the coach, but the thought of discourtesy never left their mind. Being from the South, manners and common courtesy are a big part of our culture. This may not have struck a nerve with some, but how you treat people in an everyday meal reflects how you treat them in a work setting, in casual passing, or on a football field. They completed the trip, enjoyed the campus and the city, and crossed the school off the list.

We explained to Tyson that attention to authenticity is a two-way street. Each partner in the relationship must equally attract and reciprocate. How you conduct yourself off the field is just as important and carries just as much weight as your performance on the field. Recruiters don't come to the games to see you play. They can watch film for that. They come to see how you act on the sideline, how you respond to your coaches, and how you interact with your family after the game. They want to know how you respond to adversity. Are you throwing your helmet to the ground in frustration, pouting on the bench, or blaming your teammates for a busted play? Surely, a nonproductive response will leave the scouts dumbfounded, just as Kathy stared across the table at the coach stuffing his face.

It was like night and day to compare and contrast the overall differences that Tyson and I experienced in recruitment. Because neither of my parents had attended school beyond high school, they were simply content that I was seeking higher education and did not sit down with me and evaluate the pros and cons of the dozen or so offers that I had received. They allowed my 18-year-old brain to decide on the first and only school that I had gone to visit.

Tyson sporting his new Texas Tech gear.

Be the Rolls Royce

You've probably heard of employee engagement scores derived from questionnaires and polls. Employees (anonymously) weigh in, for example, on their feelings of loyalty, satisfaction, enjoyment, and willingness to go the extra mile. This engagement helps employers retain staff by improving and elevating work environments. Employers that seek to bring value to their brand act on this feedback. They are able to entice and recruit the best of the best by offering satisfying and inspiring jobs—jobs that people compete for within a company known for being excellent. This brings recognition within industries fueled by motivated employees.

When people feel valued, they bring value. So, how would you rank yourself as an employer? A spouse? A parent? How do you engage? What makes you different? What are the things that persuade your consumers to connect with you? What are the qualities that attracted you to your soulmate? Conversely, what are the qualities that attracted you?

I was once told, "If you price yourself as a Rolls Royce, then you'll be a Rolls Royce, and if you price yourself as a Prius, then you'll be a Prius." First and foremost, this means you have to value yourself, and I mean highly. This attracts the customers you want in your business and the people you want in your life. Like attracts like, as I mentioned in *The Shopping Cart chapter*. We attract what and who we are.

As entrepreneurs, we don't settle for undercutting the competition—we want to be the competition. Valuing yourself is a crucial part of what makes you successful. What's your time worth? If you discount yourself, then you'll attract those who do not value your time or your services. Once you cheapen yourself, those individuals will continue to milk everything they can get from you. Know your worth!

Yes, know your worth, and know your product's worth. A great example and one of my favorite stories involves the CEO of Gambrinus, 46-year-old Carlos Alvarez. He grew up around the beer business and founded Gambrinus in 1986. He started in the sales department of Mexico City's Modelo brewery, which makes Corona, and worked his way up to export director in the late seventies. He started the Corona brand with a conservative price point and discovered that his beer was not selling as he imagined it would. He then decided to raise the price to match that of premium beers and noticed that his sales volume increased significantly.

So, why did this method work for him? According to social psychologist Robert Cialdini, businesses can actually increase their sales by raising prices. In a *Forbes* interview by Dorie Clark titled "How Raising Prices Can Increase Your Sales," he states, "Markets in which people are not completely sure of how to assess quality, they use price as a stand-in for quality." This tells us that consumers are willing to pay more when they believe a product is worth it. It's all about perception. The price point matched superior beers, insinuating it was a superior beer, and the Corona brand also consistently delivered quality. So Corona drinkers became fans and loyal customers of a brand they valued highly at an increased price.

By 1986, Corona became so popular that Alvarez was able to strike a deal with Modelo, break off from his employer, and establish Gambrinus to import Modelo's now-famous beer to Texas and the eastern half of the U.S. Frost Bank gave Alvarez a credit line, which he used to launch Gambrinus. In 1989, the year it acquired Spoetzl, a relatively small brewery in Shiner, Texas, Gambrinus sold $75 million worth of Corona. Then—get this—Gambrinus began marketing Shiner Bock (acquired under Spoetzl) as a specialty brew—a "handcrafted beer."

Alvarez boosted interest in Shiner Bock by gradually raising its price by $1.50 per six-pack, just below most craft brews. The story goes that Spoetzl's production skyrocketed from 35,000 barrels (one barrel equals about 330 twelve-ounce bottles of beer) in 1990 to 138,000 barrels in 1995, making Shiner Bock the best-selling Bock beer in the country.

From the time of Alvarez's brewery acquisition throughout next 10 years, production nearly tripled, all because of perception. When the public sees you as elite... top of the line... first class... the Rolls fucking Royce of your industry, then they are more likely to pay a premium for your brand, product, or service. This is enticement in a nutshell.

Be Genuine

Have compassion. Have empathy. Make each connection memorable. People intuitively know that I have their best interests at heart. I genuinely care about my patients and set them up for success. Even from the beginning, when my patient base was barely existent, and my bank account was even less existent, I didn't push big treatment plans for quicker cash flow or accelerated financial gain. I also chose to be transparent by expressing this to my patients. I wasn't trying to take their money, and I genuinely wanted to help them, which is enticing to the patients. That kind of honesty and vulnerability builds respect and trust within the relationship. This goes for any business.

Don't try to hustle people out of their money and throw them in the trash. The ideal business model is to earn customer loyalty, minimize your turnover, and get paid on the back end. Nobody wants to be sold on fast-talking, egotistical bullshit. People want to be sold on the actual product or service. Depending on your business, that could take one meeting or more than a year, but it has to be genuine every fucking time.

While growing my own business, I crossed paths with a new business owner who earned my business immediately. Josh Strack, owner of United Fitness Apparel in College Station, Texas, was just three years into his business. UFA is a company that has created a casual athletic brand and provides custom printing services of all types. In the time that I have known Josh (at the time, it was only one year), I have seen his business absolutely explode, forcing him to move to Austin to capture a larger market, all the while maintaining a personal relationship with each and every one of his customers.

Intrigued by his rapidly growing success, I sent him a text and asked, "What would you say are a few things that enabled your business to grow the way it did?"

His response:

> *Customer relations, I would say, is number one. Being approachable. Always willing to do or try something new for the customer and working relentlessly toward the end product are all things that have made us successful. To me, this shows customers that they aren't just a number on a board but that their order has a specific purpose and meaning to the company. They became important no matter how big or small an order is and no matter if it's in our own brand or customer order. Building that bond with the customer then makes a repeat customer, which turns into a referral machine. What I mean by that is if anyone around that individual is talking about having products made or wanting new gym clothes, then the individual is going to subconsciously think about us because of the good experience he or she had and*

instantly throw our name into the ring. Needless to say, you treat each and every customer in that same fashion, and you create a multiplying effect of loyal repeat customers that grows exponentially.

Wow, maybe he should actually be writing a book. This goes to show what kind of a guy he is. He could have replied back with a one-word or a single-sentence answer, but instead, he sent back a detailed explanation, and that is only about a quarter of what he wrote. I think it's very ironic that he used the word approachable. This is a professional who puts every ounce of effort into his work to accommodate the customer's expectations, and he never fails to deliver. He and I have a very similar approach to our business. Josh was later offered a dream job with Jeff Bezos's Blue Origin Aerospace Company that he just could not pass up. Sadly for us, he liquidated UFA and relocated to the Northwest for his new job.

You'll hear me talk later about gaining trust from your clientele, and this is how you do it. You have to set up your business in a way that people can easily recognize you aren't just out for their money and you actually care about them, especially if you're a small business. That is what's attractive to consumers! Tailor your business plan so that you can do exactly what the consumer is expecting and wanting from you. This is not the time to copy and paste onto an online template. Your business plan is your vision, and your vision is within you. It's what works for you and what keeps your product and your customer as the number one priority.

Appeal to Your Audience, For Better or Worse

Have you ever been to a restaurant where the service completely made the meal? A great server can make a mediocre meal seem like a phenomenal meal, just as a terrible, inattentive server can turn a gourmet meal into a one-star establishment. In my early twenties, before I started personal training, I bartended and waited tables at a lakeside restaurant and bar on Lake of the Ozarks in Missouri called Lil Rizzo's— a vacation spot with a fun, playful atmosphere. I was relatively new to the industry. I had a friend who was the assistant manager of the place and brought me on for the summer. I was a dumb, young kid making money hand over fist and spending it just as fast, but I learned some excellent lessons in customer service. People want to be taken care of, and they want to be treated like equals.

It's about your demeanor. Simple gestures got me a few extra bucks added to the tip. By using a few simple yet effective techniques, I was able to win over my tables. When I had a table of four or less (this is harder to do with a big party), I simply squatted next to the table when it came time to take orders. Squatting put me at eye level or even just a bit lower than the customers. Subconsciously, they felt better because I wasn't talking down to them, literally. In my experience, there's a psychological and social significance to this eye-level, relatable approach. Face-to-face conversations allowed me to connect with the customer on another level.

Couples came in for dates, and if they sat in a booth, I playfully scooted one of them over and sat down at the table to take the order. I was one of them at that moment, and they felt more comfortable with me. Again, the psychology of service made me successful—but there's a caveat. PLEASE be aware of where you work before trying this technique. If you do this in an upscale restaurant, then you better believe your ass is getting fired!

Again, with couples, at the end of the meal, I brought out the check and set it in front of the woman. Nine times out of ten, she'd look at me with a puzzled look on her face. I'd playfully say, "What? You're not paying?" She'd slide the check to the guy, and he'd chuckle. That chuckle just scored me a few extra bucks on the tip. Little details and simple gestures work on a much bigger scale, resulting in much bigger payoffs.

Appeal to your audience even on your worst day. Amidst your screw-ups, you can still come out on top, and you can still be enticing. Same summer, same restaurant, I was working a lunch shift. Thankfully, it was exceptionally slow on this day. I had a table of four ladies, probably mid-fifties to mid-sixties. They had just finished a round of golf and were sitting down for salad, pizza, and some drinks.

On my first trip to the table, I spilled a glass of water across the table. The ladies quickly backed away, only getting a small amount on one of the women's legs. I cleaned it up, handed the lady some extra napkins, apologized profusely, and brought another glass out. Not much later, after I brought the salads and the first round of drinks out, I reached across the table to refill a water glass and knocked over another water glass into the same lady's lap. This time it was much worse, and she was soaked.

At this point, I was completely frazzled. Mind you, I rarely spilled anything, and that was twice on this one table and on the same person. I finally got past the drinks, and it was time to bring out their pizza. Personally, this pizza was among the best I'd ever tasted. It was a thin and boasted a flaky crust. The ladies were in for quite a treat. I carried it on a serving tray and approached the table, still very shaken up. Then for some reason, I tilted my tray! The pizza slid and headed straight for the water-soaked lady. I quickly extended my arm, caught the pizza, and saved her (and myself) from another accidental mess.

I set the stand and the pizza on the table and said, "I'm so sorry, ladies. I'm clearly having a very off day. I am going to take care of your entire bill." They could see that I wasn't having a typical day, and they didn't even know me. I'm sure they deduced that if I picked up tabs on the regular for "bad days," I'd be broke as a joke. So they said it wasn't necessary and requested the ticket. I still insisted and left the table. I came back within a few minutes with their ticket, showing them it was zeroed out, and let them know that I had taken care of it. I don't remember the exact amount, but it was approximately a $75 tab. I laid it on the table, apologized one last time, wished them a great time at the lake, and went back to the kitchen.

As I returned to clean off their table, they had already left. There was a $100 bill lying there. On the back of the receipt, it read, "We all have off days. Thank you for everything."

These ladies saw that I put them number one. I wasn't out to make a quick buck, and I took pride in myself, the ultimate "end product." In other words, my presence, work ethic, care, and honesty are what the ladies took away from this encounter. They might not remember the pizza, but they will (probably) never forget the waiter who had an off day…and owned it.

Down Payment on a Cheeseburger

It takes absolutely no money to be enticing because creativity and charisma are free. That's all it takes. It's not about being in the right place at the right time. It's about strategically putting yourself in front of your desired audience and effectively getting the message across. I knew a homeless man who stood on a corner of the plaza in Kansas City with a sign that said, "I need a down payment on a cheeseburger." He put himself in a high-traffic area where people with disposable income flooded by, and he did what every other homeless person does.

He asked strangers for money or food but did it with pizazz. He didn't just have a sign that said, "Hungry, need food, God bless." He sat down and took the time to draw people in. To him, it wasn't about how many likes he could get on a post or whether he was popular or not. It was about survival. That's how you have to look at business. You have to learn to evolve with your target audience, or you'll get left out in the cold. Failure to tap into these qualities will leave you shivering, hungry, and thinking of something enticing to write on a cardboard sign, figuratively—and maybe literally.

Recently, I was leaving the grocery store with my 12-year-old son. As we exited, we heard the beautiful sound of a violin playing in the distance. I paused for a moment before crossing the parking lot to see where it was coming from. On the corner of the far aisle of the lot, a woman stood under a tree, playing her instrument for anyone who would listen. Her son sat behind her beneath the shade of the tree with his legs crossed and a clear jar sitting in his lap.

When I got into my vehicle, I sat for a moment with the windows down and the radio off. She didn't have a sign. She wasn't flagging down cars and soliciting money. She was simply sharing her unique talent with the public. The whole scene touched me to the point I exited my car and headed back to put money in the jar held by her son. Her work mattered. And despite her low-key and unobtrusive fundraising effort, her work was rewarded by me and others who soaked up her melodies and reciprocated with appreciation.

CHAPTER 5
BRICK BY BRICK

As you manage your money, you manage your life.
~ Dan Millman

So, my fellow entrepreneurs, running a business should sound considerably more pleasing than taking orders from someone else. But there's a disclaimer here: entrepreneurialism is not child's play. There is an inherent risk in branching out on your own and numerous ways to fail. I learned through trial and error, and so will you. Whereas I can't formally give you financial advice, I can help to create a framework that will allow you to build a successful and prosperous life. Brick by brick, we can increase our wealth by being purposeful throughout each phase.

If you are struggling to get to the financial position that you strive to be, then now is the opportunity for you to lay the groundwork for your short-term, intermediate, and long-term phases. The rich get richer through responsible saving and spending habits that allow them to increase their wealth at an exponential rate based on their credit and their ability to produce multiple products. That's what this chapter is all about.

If you want to own a business, consider a number of strong habits that helped me succeed. If you already own a business, these habits can help build a stronger foundation.

Before we can ever get to this point, let's address a very important, and often avoided topic—money management. Where is your money going? Do you have enough tucked away? Is your money making money for you?

Almost everyone relates to a time in life when money was a huge struggle, and some still live in that nightmare. My goal is to provide perspective as a business owner and an "aspiring to be responsible" individual who has experienced both sides of the equation. As we navigate through this chapter, we'll discuss the importance of saving, the importance of money management in building your future, and breaking your financial growth into three different periods to help determine where you are and where you should be.

When plotting out your financial timeline, you must begin with the ending in mind. Your roadmap must have a destination; otherwise, we are meandering aimlessly in nonproductive circles. If you don't know where you're going, then what's the point? En route to this destination, there must be gradual checkpoints along the way to manage your progress. These checkpoints should plot your course in a way that tells you when to really dig in and get to the next level.

Think about a bike ride. When you're in low gear, it's an easier and more leisurely ride, but you're going nowhere fast. When we increase the tension to high gear, it's much harder, but we cover more distance at a much faster pace. Your happy medium should be "What pace can I sustain to reach my goal the fastest without gassing out?" Just like the ride or your daily workout, we can interval these efforts to apply resistance at specific parts of the journey.

In the planning phases or immediately following the conception of a new venture, we'll be in high gear to conquer that crucial stretch of the ride. As these ventures become more self-sustainable, you can begin to scale back the intensity, but never let your wheels freely spin. When I look at my long-term timeline, I've created specific milestones or mile marks that instruct me when to increase my gear. Towards the end of the timeline, I have theoretically accrued enough passive income to allow me to coast out the last few years before crossing the business finish line—retirement. Instead, I use this time frame to "squeeze the juice" on the last few years of actively working. This means that although I can coast, I choose to maintain a higher gear to get the most out of my ride. If, at this point, you've set up enough passive streams to give you a great retirement and you choose to coast, then by all means, coast. It's just not my style to pull up short and leave money on the table.

When I initially started writing this chapter, I already knew the premise I wanted to cover. My efforts were to reinforce a sound outline of how we should approach money management. The biggest issue was that I am not a finance guy. I quickly realized that I had little structure or outlining, causing me to dread writing in this chapter and often avoiding it altogether. I knew that I had to tackle this obstacle head-on if I wanted to effectively get my point across, so I scheduled a meeting with a friend of mine, Robert, a financial planner.

The first 20 minutes of the meeting went straight over my head. His finance terminology was beyond my scope of knowledge, and we weren't really hitting the topic I wanted to cover. Regardless that we weren't hitting the mark, I was still intently engaged and attempting to soak up any knowledge that he had to offer, all while writing like a madman in my notebook to reference later.

He paused to take a sip of his coffee, and at that moment, I said, "This is all great, but we just aren't getting what I need." He let me speak for a few minutes and explained the concepts more clearly. At that point, it all came together. He said, "I've done many talks on how to be responsible with finances. I like to break it down into three categories: short-term, intermediate-term, and long-term."

Boom! Just like that, we had structure. I was able to sit down and literally draw out an outline to this chapter with the three terms posing as the main points. The content already written was tweaked and placed into each section accordingly. This gave me the visuals I needed to make significant headway in tackling my most challenging chapter.

But remember our bike ride! Each term presents different obstacles or objectives. Some will require us to push more than others. We push harder in the beginning to allow ourselves a leisurely ride in the end.

Let's start mapping out our ride to see what it looks like.

Short Term

Naturally, we'll start in the short-term phase of saving, where we embrace the grind. You're going to work, and you're going to work hard. This is the first step of saving. Everything that you work for will form in the short-term phase. This is the concrete slab you pour for your extravagant home, and this foundation needs to be solid.

I grew up in a middle-upper-class blue-collar family. My family worked hard for everything we had. My sister and I never went without, and we never saw the struggle. My father worked shift work until I graduated high school to provide what we needed. My mother worked a nine-to-five office job, starting low and consistently working her way up the ranks.

My parents were good examples of hard workers. After long hours on the job, they came home, maintained an organized house, and often (sometimes too often) added extra projects and tasks to our chores. If my father wanted to build a fence around the backyard, change the oil a thousand miles before the recommendation on the sticker, or do some unnecessary landscaping, then I was expected to be his shadow. Usually, my helping equated to holding tools and getting yelled at, but I was expected to help, nonetheless. They put in the man hours, made their paychecks, and lived well within their means.

As I said, my father worked shifts throughout my childhood as a dragline operator at a coal mine. With nearly an hour commute each way, he worked his ass off on 12-hour shifts. The mine shut down, leaving him waiting for an opening at another mine an hour in the opposite direction. In the meantime, he started building decks and fences on the side. He looked at it as if he wasn't physically working, he wasn't making money. He had not yet mastered what we'll discuss in the *Being Passive* chapter.

Of course, any time that I wasn't in school or playing in a sporting event, I was there as his free labor. I remember one particular evening when he was working hard to complete a fence before dark. We were coming up at dusk during a day following a good rain, and the mosquitoes were absolutely atrocious. Anyone who has been to Texas knows that the mosquito is practically the state bird. They are huge! That did not deter my father from finishing the job. I vividly remember him bent over, nailing in the bottom of a picket, and his back was engulfed in a swarm of blood-harvesting mosquitoes. There was literally one on every square inch of his back, like a feeding frenzy.

He swatted and tugged at his shirt but didn't want to stop. We finished, and while it may not seem like an extravagant story, it left a lasting impression due both to the dedication to the job and the fact that you have to be physically present to make the money. The value of a dollar to him is working through unfavorable conditions to provide for his family. It was embracing the grind to start building the foundation of net worth. This is what Dad did well.

What I learned during my childhood is that the more you work, the more money you'll make. I was completely oblivious to what went on behind the scenes, though. Were my parents investing? I had no clue. What was the hierarchy of their budgeting priorities? No one talked about it. I was also completely detoured from the "work smarter, not harder" mantra. No, I was exposed to slogans like "Never stop! Never give up! The moment you relax is the moment you'll lose everything!" While being a hard worker is absolutely necessary, like I mentioned in the bike ride analogy, you can only sustain the high-gear pace for so long before it becomes undoable.

I absolutely understood the value of a dollar and what it meant to grind. Work harder than the man next to you, and you shall reap the benefits. It's the best man for the job-type shit. This is what I love about the sport of wrestling. There were no politics, and there was no relying on others to help you out. It's just you against your opponent. The most skilled who goes hardest wins. I am still that way today in business. I'm determined to outwork the competition and come out on top every time. This mentality gave me the discipline to become very diligent in my money management strategies. Although that was not always the case in my twenties, it was there when I needed it in my thirties—a very useful tool in the tool belt.

While my parents seemed very conservative in their spending habits, at this point, I was not briefed on the importance of what to do with my earnings. Like most children, I thought money was best spent on the newest toy or game console. But how will we ever grow if we are constantly sitting on zero? It's substantially more important to know what to do after the grind because, honestly, the grind is the easy part. Everyone can work, but what is done after the grind when your money hits your account is what sets the elite apart from the rest of the world.

Our ability to save our money will determine the outcome of our successes. This skill should be learned (or taught) at a young age. If you strive to be a successful individual yet lack the ability to keep money in your pocket, step one is to do whatever you must to learn this skill. If you're a parent, failure to teach your children responsibilities is a surefire way to lead them down the road of disappointment, struggle, and failure. Regardless of whether you have children or not, this is a good time to reflect on what money-saving habits you are implementing in your life. Knowing what bucket to distribute your money into will ultimately gauge the pace of your growth. With that being said, we have to grasp success-promoting decisions about where to distribute our money. This revolves around a fundamental process guiding you to the next opportunity. We do not want to begin "digging the financial hole" early in life. It is hell getting out of that proverbial hole. Are you poised in your saving abilities and driven to succeed? Are you confident in the path that you're on? Most importantly, are you applying your money to productive sources that are congruent with your timeline?

In the summer of 2023, I began networking at the Bryan/College Station chapter of 1,000,000 Cups, a networking event that brings local entrepreneurs together in order to grow local businesses within the community. In doing so, I reconnected with another financial planner I knew by the name of Will. He became the fine-tooth comb who looked over this chapter one last time before it published. He told me that rather than using chronological terms, he set up his clients' portfolios by the potential return of the investment. He broke his investment categories up into conservative, aggressive, and home run. While Will took a different approach in structuring things, the two strategies actually align themselves very well. We just have to know which type of investment to apply to which term.

While it would be so nice to tee up the home run ball in the short term, for most of us it's just not logical. Home run investment typically comes from big boy capital and very likely has big boy risk attached to it. If we have not established our savings and emergency funds, then we have nothing to fall back on. Like our equitable growth, we stairstep our conservative investments to gain some steam.

All right, let's look back to where this mentality derives. It comes from the traits your parents and your mentors instilled in you. What characteristics did your parents instill in order for you to be a winner? How did they teach you responsibility? In the short term, your safest investment is in stockpiling whatever you can so that the next term can be much more profitable. Thus, we save our money. In this example, I needed not only to be reminded to save my earnings but how to save my earnings. I know it's easy to say, "Save your money," but when it comes down to it, how many of us were actually taught how to follow through? How do we continually shovel money into our savings account when that brand-new pair of sunglasses just hit the market (sunglasses are my weakness)?

According to both of my resources, the short term was explained to me as funds that are needed immediately, being savings and emergency money. We need these accounts to act as a safety net when unavoidable instances occur, such as your car breaking down, you losing your job, someone getting sick and can't work, or you need to take care of dependents, whatever it may be. These funds will be available to cover these expenses without putting yourself in a financial bind.

Now that we have established the use of this money, let's get back to saving and how we can accomplish this. Imagine yourself starting from scratch. You have nothing, and this is your starting point. You have a blank canvas to work with, and starting with a strong foundation in your short-term savings plan will provide infinite potential to create a masterpiece of a financial portfolio.

How Zero Balance Really Works

Throughout college and into my first marriage, I constantly teetered between the black and red in my account. I was handcuffed into only being capable of purchases that the value of a dollar could support, the often minuscule number that was sitting in my bank account.

It wasn't until I created the sliding scale of a "zero balance" that I really started saving my money. The principle ultimately teaches you how to save. For people like me who thrive on competition and reaching goals, it forced me to build my account through a stair-step process of achieving smaller, incremental goals. Here is how the "zero balance" works. A true zero balance is zero. If you fall below that, you're in the negative, and you're most likely paying some fees associated with that lack of responsibility. Set your zero balance to what is achievable for you at that time. Start off small and make $500 your new zero balance. If at any point you fall below this number, then you're in the red. Whatever you set the amount at should be an amount that you can maintain over the period of at least three months. It is not realistic to set your amount prior to paying any expenses that may dip your account below your new zero balance. Account for these expenses ahead of time.

If your monthly expenses are $2000, then set the $500 zero balance when you're comfortably hitting $2500 in your bank account. That way, at the end of the month when all of your financial obligations have been processed, you're still sitting pretty in the black. Once you've successfully maintained this new balance for three months and have been able to save on top of that, then reevaluate your financial position and reset your zero balance to a new but still attainable balance and work towards that.

When I say attainable, I mean something that can be accomplished within the next few months. Remember, this is still the short term. It is not realistic to say, "Okay, I am going to save $20,000 and buy a house!" without growing into it. People who work to save their money in order to put a down payment on a house or a car do so incrementally. This is the time to really apply those SMART goals by George Doran—"Smart, Measurable, Attainable, Realistic and Time-based." The 20 grand is a good goal, but it has no end date and is not realistic at this point in the game. Our next set, "zero balance," is something like $750 or $1000.

It is challenging, yes, but absolutely achievable. If we baby-step it the entire way, you can expect to reach that $20,000 when you're retiring, but even with this modest example, we would be hitting $20,000 at the ten-year mark. Remember, as you accumulate money and maintain productive saving habits, your equitable growth will typically grow in a snowball fashion. Each revolution of the snowball down the mountain (although we are traveling upwards) will essentially double the size, increasing the momentum to build your empire much quicker.

To clarify, your equitable growth is money saved but separate from your savings account. Your equitable growth represents the value of your business or your brand. If you're not a business owner, then the brand is you. Your equitable growth provides capital for what you're plotting in your business plan. It's created to provide capital for future business endeavors and retirement scenarios. Your savings account is personal, and although we start building this account in the short term, it is for our long-term benefit. Once you've hit the $1000 for three months consecutively, increase the number again, but never allow yourself to fall into the red, meaning we stay above our new perceived bottom line. Using this method will promote continuous growth and bring awareness of your endeavors and, also, spending habits. You'll begin to realize that as you stay consistent in sustaining your zero balance, your ability to do so will become easier, almost effortless.

Look at it this way. We are essentially building a house with the graph and are plotting with our financial data. Every house has a floor, a roof, and walls/living space. Now we have established the floor to our new home, our zero balance. Before we talk about the contents of the house, let's put a roof on it. Traveling in a similar upward trend, at a balance obviously higher than your new zero balance, is your total

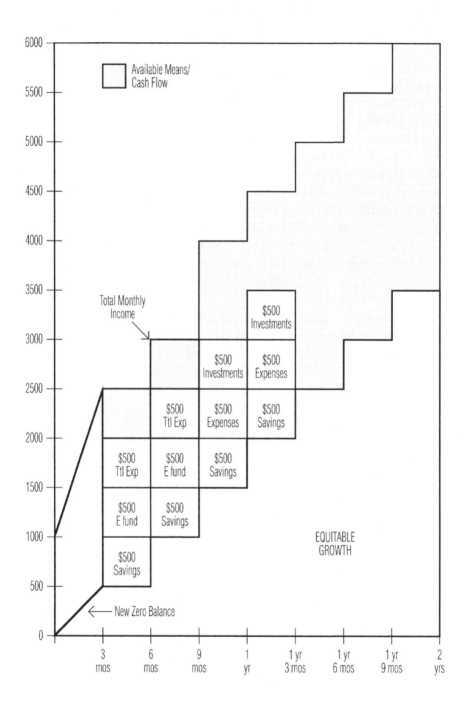

monthly income. Now is a good time to reference the preceding graph, which allows you to build your financial "house" in real time, and follow along throughout the chapter. Between these two lines is your "living space." In terms of this example, you're a hermit, and you're staying home.

Both numbers should gradually increase; however, if they don't, no worries! You're still accumulating equitable growth below your new zero balance. That's not ideal, though. We are always shooting for an upward trend. Your total monthly income is directly reflected by your will to grind, but it does not determine the value of your brand. The value of your brand resides below the new zero balance line. We cannot determine the value of the brand by the total income line due to expenses, both productive and nonproductive, being pulled from this amount. The short term is very much associated with the value of the dollar while learning strong saving habits and smart spending habits to build our credit and allow for greater surges in our income in the intermediate term.

Our strong saving habits and responsible money management will allow us to build credit to act as a catalyst in rapidly multiplying our net worth. All of the money we have saved is great, but it is limited to the current dollar amount in your account. In the simplest terms, the value of a dollar is limited to the exact amount that you have at any moment in time, whether it be cash or in an investment account of some sort. If you have no credit, you're limited to just that. However, if you have good credit, just as he said, the credit can be diversified into different areas to increase your overall net worth.

For example, you may not have $400,000 in your bank account at a particular time, but if you have credit and the income to qualify, you can use that credit to purchase a $400,000 home. If you have no credit at all, your only option would be to pay the entire $400,000 in cash, eliminating any liquid assets you have accumulated, tying all of your wealth into one property and limiting your access to that asset only by selling it. It is important to remember that credit is best used to invest in appreciating assets, though.

Assets such as vehicles, recreational items, or personal items such as jewelry tend to depreciate and therefore do nothing to increase your overall wealth. Remember that your net worth is not determined by a status symbol, as people tend to believe with luxury cars or designer clothes. We'll discuss this later in the chapter with investments and consumption.

When we look at it from a small business point of view, unless you have the cash to fund the entire start-up capital and about a year of operating capital, then you'll need credit. Credit gives you the ability to pay for all of the initial borrowed capital for startup over time while also offering you the ability to make money to pay off what was borrowed. It also created additional wealth for yourself. Ideally, the value of the business is increasing while the amount of debt is decreasing, none of which would be possible without credit. This all sounds great on paper, but the steps to get there can be tedious. They can also be treacherous if we are not implementing good saving habits, paying off principle early, and allowing interest to consume our hard-earned money.

There is the "necessary evil" of opening various lines of credit because it's the only way that we can build our trust with creditors, but they must be handled with extreme care. These lines of credit can benefit or hurt your credit score, and this is all based on how you manage them. I would go as far as saying that the value of credit and the value of a dollar are directly related. When we utilize productive saving habits, distribute our finances appropriately, and have awareness of our spending, our cash flow will naturally increase, but also our credit score. Inversely, if we neglect these habits of depreciating items and poor financial habits, both values will, in turn, also depreciate.

Now that we have discussed how we should be saving our money and its effect on our credit, it's time to discuss our expenses. We'll grow most of our accounts in relative fashion, incrementally stair-stepping our new zero balance and our total monthly income. Four categories remain constant, maybe not in amounts, but instead they will always reside within the living area of your growth chart.

The first of these is establishing our total monthly expenses you're obligated to (outside of the other categories that we'll discuss shortly), as the remainder of our financial decisions will initially be determined by this figure. We have already acknowledged that this figure is also the determinant of setting our initial zero balance. Everything that recurrently requires financial fuel to allow your life to operate will fall into this category: rent or mortgage, utilities, student loans, business loans, business operating costs, car payments, gas, phone, dog food, household items, everything. This category is self-explanatory but is one that can get away from us without strict spending and saving habits.

Reclaim yourself from the creature of habit and plot out every expense that is deducted from your bank account. It doesn't matter how big or small; it needs to be accounted for. A new pair of shoes for $150? Mark it down. An overpriced $5 latte at the coffee shop? Yep, that too. These are the expenses that will eat you up and send your stack through the roof of your living area.

The second category is the emergency fund, the primary, or focal, account of the short term. The emergency fund is set up to assure we'll move in a positive direction in the event of an emergency. Accidents happen, people get sick, and jobs get lost, so we must prepare accordingly for the unforeseeable. Quoting Dave Ramsey, a highly reputable source, "The emergency fund should be based on expenses and should be capable of covering 3-6 months of your expenses."

For this example, let's go with three months of our listed expenses. The numbers should reflect you as single or you as a family. We mentioned earlier that we cannot invest in depreciating assets; however, we use the emergency fund to cover calculated expenses on depreciating necessities. Our vehicles will depreciate, and we realize that we'll be obligated to purchase a new one in the future. Roofs begin to leak, mattresses exceed their lifespan, and washing machines break. It is much easier to incrementally and gradually acquire the funds to cover these occurrences rather than scramble to get it at the last minute.

Earlier, I threw out the figure of $2000 as our monthly overhead, so we'll go with that number again. With this figure in place, we have to grow our emergency fund to a capability of covering $6,000 of living expenses. Assuming that we stay well within our "living space," we'll set our monthly contribution to the emergency fund at $500. With this rate of entry, we can assume that we'll meet our cap at the end of one year.

After we have accumulated our necessary funds, the emergency fund will no longer receive funds, and one of three things will occur. One, you'll now take the amount that was funneled into the emergency fund and instead add it to your new zero balance, more rapidly increasing your equitable growth. Two, apply that amount to your personal savings to increase your personal growth. Or three, you'll implement an investment account as the premise of the intermediate term, so it will be discussed there.

Next, we'll discuss the savings account. As mentioned earlier, the savings account represents personal growth, and unlike the emergency fund, there is no cap on this account. There may be a sliding scale of entry, or it may remain constant. Although it would be easier to maintain a consistent amount being distributed into this account each month, I would highly recommend that we have a sliding scale of entry so as to directly reflect the increase in our total monthly income.

In the sliding scale of entry, we assess the total income to determine what amount per month you can afford to funnel into your savings and set it up on a recurring transaction. The new zero balance has no determining factor of the growth of entry into your savings, or your emergency fund, for that matter. When using the sliding scale of entry for your savings, it should be traveling at a congruent rate of growth as your income.

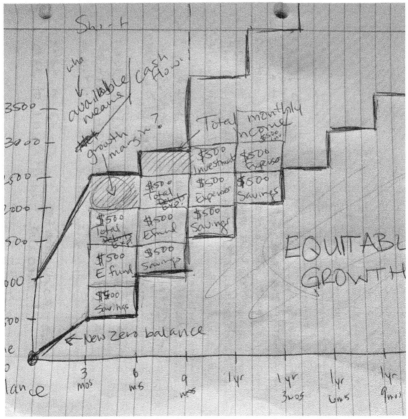

Rough draft of what I wanted the graph to look like.

As you can see in the chart, the emergency fund and the savings account sit atop the total monthly expenses within the living space. We'll call this your "stack." Your chart should have been thoroughly thought out and set up to allow for a gap between the top of your stack and the line representing your total monthly income. The larger this gap, the more financial freedom we have in our lives. Within this gap sits our available means. After all our obligations have been met, and all monthly distributions have been made, this is what is left over.

The decisions that you make of the use of these available means will show the productivity of your growth. A breakdown of the available means will be presented in the following term. This is a good time to sit down, figure out your monthly expenses, set your zero balance, determine monthly contributions to your emergency fund and savings account, and begin building your future. Your short term is coming to an end, and it's time to start making some real dough in the intermediate term.

Intermediate Term

Now that we've learned how to save, we move into the intermediate term. This is where we embrace the hustle. This is the true time of growth. The distributions that we initially experienced in the savings phase begin to take shape as we apply them to investments. We begin to accumulate wealth by giving ourselves opportunities and preparing for the future.

In this term, we strive to increase the gap of our available means for two main purposes: one, to cover all calculated expenses that we'll face in the future, and two, to allow for more investment freedom to skyrocket our net worth. As I said, this term is the true time of growth, and your decision on how to apply the available means will determine the rate of that growth. Now that this has been established, we move further into increasing our net worth.

Through strong saving habits in the short term, we are already showing responsibility to potential lenders. However, as we begin implementing the fourth and final category into the stack—the investment fund—we'll really need to begin focusing on your credit. This category in the stack is what we pull from to fund smaller recurring investments, such as stocks, bonds, cryptocurrencies, mutual funds, real estate investments, etc. These are what Will would call your "aggressive" investments—posing moderate risk to yield moderate to high reward.

Depending on your investment timeline, this will determine how aggressively we begin channeling funds into your investment fund, whereas your equitable growth is at a slow steady pace. Upon investing in new endeavors, new zero balances will be established for those brands, operating simultaneously yet independently; however, all brands may funnel into the same investment account. More simply, each business or expansion to a business that you start will have its own zero balance and its own rate of equitable growth. With that being said, slowly growing five zero balances will create future capital for new endeavors at a substantially faster rate than only growing one. Note, our investment fund will be directed primarily at aggressive investments, allowing us to increase our zero balance faster and growing our equitable growth at a faster rate, which is primarily what we are using for our home run investments.

In this term, we utilize our investment fund, which is amplified by the excess amount of our available means, and our superior credit to begin investing in new endeavors. The return on investment (ROI), as we progress through this term, should continually replenish and grow your investment fund to fully subsidize all subsequent endeavors. Very typically, as we grow as a business, these endeavors will substantially grow as well. The equitable growth below your growing zero balance is there for your larger investments. As this number grows, along with the ever-growing investment fund supplying it, it will provide you with the capital to apply towards our "home run" investments, such as business startups, higher-end/commercial real estate, and investments that yield major returns. Once you've caught a marlin, there is not much pleasure in reeling in a perch, right? Whereas we may be capable of supporting a favorable portion of the next marlin investment, it is very likely that credit will be needed to cover the rest. Always thinking optimistically never let your marlin idea be deterred by a perch budget, but with the strategic management that we've demonstrated thus far, we should be good. Feed it and grow it, until it's your baby and you're proud to hang it over the mantle.

Our investments in this term act as the potential energy for your long-term financial situation to swell tremendously.

One of my favorite questions is, "What would you do if you won the lottery?" If you say anything other than "Immediately invest and continue working," then close this book now. You have just thrown away your fortune.

How do we know what we should invest in? There are four components I use when investing for myself: Invest in what you know, invest in what you're passionate about, calculate your ROI, and know when to pull the trigger. As I stated earlier, I personally trained for 10 years prior to getting into chiropractic. The schedule for a personal trainer typically exists outside of the normal nine-to-five schedule. I was getting up at 4:30 a.m. every morning to train in the overly common 5:30 a.m. workout spot, maybe train a midmorning group of stay-at-home soccer moms, network throughout the day while my family was at work and school, get my workout in, then train in the evenings. I was not getting the time that I needed with my kids. I love training, but not as much as I love my family.

In the summer of 2011, I was teaching a boot camp at a local park for a group of clients. One particular day, I had a client whom I had been training for years, Kellie, show up to a class hunched over and holding her mid back in anguish. At that time I knew essentially nothing about chiropractic, but having superior knowledge of the body, I told her, "Just lay on this mat and let me see what I can do." I proceeded to stand over her and press through her mid back, providing some soft tissue release and mobilizing her hips and spine, relieving her pain. She looked up at me and said, "Wow, that was as good as my normal chiropractor." I know, I know. I never should have done that, but that moment changed my life forever.

Knowing that I was burning out on the hours of personal training and putting my family on the back burner, I researched chiropractic schools and the criteria to get in. I knew it was time to pull the trigger, and the rest is history. I discovered there was a chiropractic school within fifteen minutes of my house, so I toured the school, applied, and got in. After my nearly four-year investment, I graduated with my doctorate in chiropractic. A little over a year following our day in the park, Kellie and her family moved away, putting an end to our workouts. Needless to say, just following graduation, I contacted Kellie and thanked her for changing my life. That one day brought light on what direction I needed to take my life, and I chose it. It was time to transition to my intermediate term.

I knew that in this term, I'd accrue substantial debt to invest in my future, but I also knew that the return on my investment would supersede the amount of that debt and make for a better life. While this story relates more to investing in myself and very similar to my decision to move from mid-Missouri to Kansas City, it demonstrates the four components of how I invest.

One hindering fact remained; I spent much of my short term in a dopamine frenzy, doing nothing for my credit score and leaving me with fewer options to get started in the professional world. As I got into business, I heavily relied on my family to get me through the loan process. I needed more good credit, and I needed more collateral to allow me to do the things that I needed to do to be successful. It was necessary for me to take out a business loan to make the business work.

Because I had poor to average credit, I had no other option than to have my parents cosign and put up collateral to get the loan approved. My family is at the point where they are well into the intermediate term, making investments to further enrich their lives before transitioning into the long term. While helping me did not deplete their abilities to continue moving forward, what they had tied up in my business did inhibit them from investing to their full potential.

When you're unable to subsidize your own endeavors, you have two options: you can either wait it out until you're capable of making the move, or you can acquire support from an outside source. If you're going to wait it out, the question you must ask yourself is, *Can I make the necessary changes in my life to get to the place that allows me to do what I want on my own?* With this, you're in a race. You're not only against yourself, but you're racing against inflation, fast-rising taxes, and rapidly evolving competition.

If you need $50,000 for the endeavor now and it takes you five years to get to where you need to be, then you can anticipate needing a minimum of $60,000 to complete the same task that you want to do today. Acquiring outside help will increase your stress due to the increasing number of people involved. If you have good credit and the collateral to match the loan, it is just you and the creditor. When an investor is brought in, you're now responsible for reimbursing the creditor and the investor(s). More mouths to feed and more hands reaching into the cookie jar equates to more stress.

Increased Credit = Decreased Stress

Now progressing through a successful business, these moves begin to get easier. I essentially had a merging of my short-term and intermediate-term in my first two years in business to put myself in a comfortable position. This isn't easy, but it is achievable. Money and credit have both been elevated to a comfortable level, allowing me to engage freely in new investments that will continue to grow my net worth.

It's funny how getting some positive momentum can change your outlook on life. Your eyes open, and suddenly, your objective in life has a new meaning. Tomorrow becomes now, and you begin investing in your life and your future. The decisions that you make to protect your pursuit of greatness become more abundant. Things like life insurance take the place of ordering bottle service at the nightclub to ensure being the life of the party. These bad decisions that we seemingly make in the infancy of our success begin to dissipate and shift into a more responsible realm. Now you can comfortably afford the $300 bottle service, but you choose to apply those funds to a more productive source.

This may be why we have a bigger bank account now. These petty, pretentious things no longer matter in the grand scheme of things. Maybe John from *The Shopping Cart* would have gotten here faster if he had recognized that his toxic decisions were hurting him two-fold: money and credit. Our growth in the available means is directly related to our ability to control our consumption versus investment. Consumption is the bottle service to liven the party, the designer clothes that make us *feel* like a million bucks, or the luxury car that runs exactly the same as its little sister company's counterpart.

The way that I look at this situation is the difference between adsorbent and absorbent. One letter that makes all the difference in the world. Imagine for a moment a dry sponge and a normal piece of standard computer paper. We also have two twelve-ounce glasses of water sitting on two separate tables. We take each of the glasses and pour the water out onto the tables. In one puddle, we place the sponge. The sponge is absorbent. It represents an individual who applies the available means as an investment. The water quickly absorbs into the sponge, filling it and causing it to grow, much like the individual who practices responsible habits. This individual will avoid vanity and impulsive habits that prevent his growth. The permeability of the sponge and "absorbent" mindsets allow us to grow at a rapid rate.

On the other puddle, we place the sheet of paper. The paper is quite the opposite, representing our more consumption-oriented individuals. It is adsorbent, causing the water to adhere to the outer surface of the object, much like the flashy appearance of the pretentious person, but never promoting growth, only the appearance of it. The paper appears to be shiny, but it does not hold any weight. Not only are we not growing, but we are also leaving behind a lot of water on the table. All of the leftover water is potential growth. All of the leftover water is what you should be applying to your equitable growth, growing your investment fund, or stockpiling for your retirement.

Let's look at these ounces of water and pretend that they are money. Of the twelve ounces, only two of them are necessary to live. While the sponge absorbs all twelve ounces, it expands, holding on to the other ten to be rung out into a quickly growing bank account. At best, the sheet of paper will collect four ounces, using two to live and the other two for the appearance of living well. These types of habits will lower both your credit and your savings. Are these unnecessary expenses taking away from your potential?

The decision to apply more of our available means to practicality will make kings of us all. Practicality yields steady growth. This doesn't mean that we can simply never splurge, but like anything, within moderation. Also, ask if this financial decision enriched your life. Is the extra $10,000 that you put on the luxury car going to give you ten grand more in satisfaction than the essentially same vehicle that you could be driving? **A pretentious mindset only acquires depreciating assets.**

Now, with visions of the future, it's time to start thinking about retirement. The road to a comfortable retirement starts now. Every day that we choose convenience and careless spending over responsibility and practicality is just that much comfort we'll lack in our later years. I'm not saying you can't enjoy the journey, but you're going to want the added comfort when you get there. Be mindful and appreciative of all that you encounter, but do not sacrifice your retirement. Once I reached a level of comfortability in my life, I began to set bigger goals for retirement—something we often overlook in our earlier years.

We'll discuss my financial goals in a while, but what about my freedom to spend time with my family, making memories that will never depreciate? That's important to me, too. It holds a lot of weight. I've set a timeline to incrementally taper back my work week every five years and have enough ducks in a row to allow myself to retire at age 50. This doesn't mean that I'm not working. This just means that I'm not physically working.

I absolutely love what I do, but it takes a toll on my body, and I have to keep the machine running. And dammit, I have to dress up for work. I'd rather be consulting, investing, and growing my worth from the comfort of my beach house, lounging around in my workout clothes with the ambient bliss of my future grandkids running around. This is where, for the sake of the book, we bookend our intermediate term.

Long Term

Upon retirement, we shift into the long term. This is where we embrace life and is the time for wealth accumulation. Everything that we had worked to save in the short term and everything that we worked to grow in the intermediate term has come to fruition now. We should enter this term with no foreseeable obligations. The beach house with our grandkids running around? Paid off. The practical cars that we bought along the way? Paid off. We should have no unnecessary debts lingering out there as we make this transition. This should be a time of enjoyment and peace.

Let's discuss wealth accumulation. You're probably thinking, *I thought I already made myself wealthy throughout the last term?* Well, now it's time for the grand finale. We enter our long term, dismissing any government-funded retirement packages and looking solely at what we have accumulated over the short and intermediate terms. Remember the sliding zero balance? The example provided was an extremely modest addition of $500 per quarter. If we spent 30 years in the intermediate term fully utilizing this system, then our zero balance, our equitable growth, would be at $60,000. This, along with our yearly revenue, shows the worth of our business.

When it's time to finally pull the trigger on retirement, we begin to look at these numbers to sell. Over the course of the last five years in business, let's say your average yearly net profit was $500,000. A good formula is taking triple the net profit over those five years and your equitable growth to determine your sellout amount.

**Average yearly net profit ($500,000) x 3 +
Equitable growth ($60,000) = Sellout ($1,560,000)**

Many of you are wondering, *How am I supposed to fund an elaborate and enjoyable retirement with only that amount of money?* Do not overlook the modesty of this example, and if we are true entrepreneurs, then this should be one of many sellout formulas that you're putting together. The objective is to create synergies from all ventures that allow us to prosper greatly in our retirement. You also have to take into consideration the field you're proposing the valuation in.

If you also remember, we are also transferring $500 per month into our savings account. After 30 years, without growing this amount, we would have a savings of $180,000. So simply between the formula that we just put together and our savings, we are sitting at $1,740,000. This example is completely void of any interest you're accruing along the way and only one of the multiple money streams we are cashing out. When buying a business, we'll strive to make that 3x amount (what we are trying to sell a business at) into 1.5–2x that five-year average of the business's net profit. Some businesses will yield a higher multiplier. It really depends on the field.

CHAPTER 6
BE A PROBLEM SOLVER

Success is neither magical nor mysterious.
Success is the natural consequence of consistently applying
the basic fundamentals.
~ Jim Rohn

Who a person is directly reflects where they are in life. We touched on it in *The Shopping Cart*. Remember the bar patrons who refused to make the changes to succeed? One of the hardest things for people to do in their lives is to figure out the process of their lives. In every person, a driving force begins to carve out a specific path they will follow. Everyone is conditioned to operate in a certain way.

Whether it is personal or professional adversity, our brains are wired to respond to those stimuli in a very specific manner. It is up to you, the individual, to control those behaviors or begin applying environmental modifications to adapt and regulate your own process. The faster we can figure out what works for us, the faster that we can be truly successful.

For some, it just clicks, and then there are those who take a while longer. What are the obstacles that cause us to deviate from our plan? Is it simply our attitude? Is it friction from an outside stimulus? Is it a conditioned response? As adults, we often catch ourselves acting out the same behaviors that our parents demonstrated. How often do you think to yourself, *I sound just like my father* or *I am doing things just like my mother did?* It is ingrained in us. It is up to you to correct course and carve your own path through life. You're conditioned to operate a particular way, but don't be misled into perpetuating the wrong responses and actions.

We all know that person who has excuses for everything going wrong or relies on someone else to help get them through life. Lost your job? "Oh, my boss sucks, and that job wasn't for me." Divorced for the third time? "She was toxic, just like my last wife." Credit card debt out of control? "Oh, it was a good sale, and a splurge makes me feel better."

No. You own your circumstances. The buck stops here. You're responsible for your triumphs and your tragedies. Taking ownership and responsibility for this thing called "life" is what a true successor does. Our ancestors battled through problems bigger than ours, and they lived long enough to pass down strong genes...survivor genes. Reach within yourself and access their mindset, determination, discipline, and self-control, and you can pull yourself out of any well.

Back to the workplace. Remember, there's a difference between relying on someone to do your work and delegating a task, which we'll discuss in the *Being Passive* chapter. Be in control of your own shit! There's no one else in this world who is going to do it for you, and there is no time for codependency.

Yoda said it best: "Do or do not. There is no try." I would say that "try" is the single word I hate the most in the English language. It makes me cringe. If I tell an employee to do something and they reply "Okay, I'll try," that means it definitely won't get done. We're not trying, we are working at it or working towards it. Change your vocabulary, change your subconscious thinking, and you'll change the outcome.

If you've ever paid attention to an experienced baseball outfielder, then you know he's confident in his abilities to get to the ball. He quickly makes an accurate judgment of the ball's trajectory and projected landing spot. He then commits or plays it on the bounce. Just because we play it on the bounce doesn't mean that we gave up on the ball. It is a part of using good judgment to know when to pursue and when to have patience. If you're not confident in your ability to get to the ball, then you'll be timid in your approach; you'll get short-hopped, and it'll pass you by.

It's the same concept when you're problem-solving. You have to commit to solving the problem in front of you. You cannot "try" to solve the problem; otherwise, the problem will never actually get resolved. I mentioned the Dave Ramsey quote earlier, stating, "Our goal is not to raise good kids, but great adults." Teaching your children at a young age to be problem solvers is a catalyst to them achieving this goal, the same goes for your employees.

A prominent quality I seek in a new employee is the ability to take initiative and tackle a problem head-on. If a problem is continuously nagging, then find a different solution. Albert Einstein stated that the definition of insanity is doing the same actions over and over again and expecting a different outcome. If you're constantly living in a revolving door of disappointment, then what part of your process is malfunctioning?

I have a friend who constantly complains about various aspects of his life, but when it comes time to make the necessary changes to allow himself to get ahead, he continues complaining about it. I explained to him that, although difficult, he had to take action and make those changes for his life to take a different course. I said, "I feel like you're banging your head against a wall and getting a headache. The wall will not get softer, so it's you who has to change."

Do not dwell on all that can go wrong or all that is currently going wrong, as it will only manifest failure as the outcome. Recognize the hurdle, then adapt and conquer. In the example of my friend, he was approaching his problems with a defensive mindset, simply reacting to the problems that life threw at him with little to no action. Action provides traction. You have to tackle problems head-on.

The Problem Solvers

Typically, problem solvers are those who are in charge because they can handle the stresses of life. On the flip side, we have those who fail to take initiative and sit idle in a puddle of helplessness. These individuals play the role of the victim. It's someone else's fault that they aren't succeeding every fucking time. It's a critical thinking error to assume that things will always run smoothly. Life is rarely perfect.

Mark Manson said, "Life is essentially an endless series of problems." This is why we are innately hardwired to tackle hardships and overcome. It's just a matter of accessing the lessons and putting them to use. It's a matter of learning from the past and doing better. Individuals who acknowledge hardships as problem-solving opportunities are the ones who prevent the same error from being made in the future. They lead the pack. It's a natural progression. You'll see in the *Obstacles* chapter that life is constantly throwing you curveballs. Not only will the strong survive, but the strong-willed will survive.

Are you complaining about other people's success? Do you frequently say, "Oh, I don't have the money to do that." Are you always searching for the "grass is greener" job? The bigger, better deal? Do you end up back at square one every time you start getting ahead? I know it's a real bitch to hear, but maybe it's you. Maybe you're the common denominator.

It's probably time to sit down and take a personal inventory of the qualities that push you ahead and also the traits that set you back. People who have a broke mentality will always be broke. They'll always be chasing the rainbow and never make it to the pot of gold. I especially see this in our youth. We are currently in an era of entitlement. The problem with entitlement is the inability to work at and solve a problem.

You cannot be the victim and be successful. Are you going to be the victim, or are you going to figure it out and take the steps necessary to climb the metaphorical ladder? Will you focus on your goals? Honor your goals?

Here's an interesting analogy. As much as we don't like to look at it this way, life is a food chain. You either eat or you don't eat. Or, in the example that I am about to give, you either eat or you get eaten. Where do you fall in line? Only you can determine your position in the feeding frenzy. Are you a problem solver or are you a victim? You can only be one.

Chris Kyle once said, "There are three types of people in this world: sheep, wolves, and sheepdogs." His famous statement strongly resonates with me and others for many reasons, especially when I think of business settings. I suggest that the goal is to be the sheepdog. Not the sheep. Not the wolf. Yet the vast majority of people in the world are sheep, and they have a definite role in society. After all, where would we be if there were no cogs in the wheel?

However, you're probably reading this book because the thought of being a sheep makes you uncomfortable. It's not how you're hardcoded. You're meant for a role outside of the herd. You aren't afraid, unlike many around us who fear just about everything—every media headline, every new societal disaster, and every uncertain situation. If you feel compelled to do more and be more, then you're either called to be a sheepdog or a wolf.

Victim = Sheep

From a wider perspective, we can compare victims to sheep. A sheep goes nowhere on its own. It's herded here and there or torn apart by the big bad wolf...that is, unless a sheepdog is nearby. If you're a complacent sheep, not wanting responsibility and happy with your place in the herd, then you're dependent on a sheepdog that saves you from your own vulnerabilities, namely, falling off cliffs or being eaten alive by a predator. Look at it this way. A sheep's happy place, its safe spot, hinges on something other than itself because it struggles to survive independently.

Mindset is an incredible thing. It's something that is hardwired into our being from an early age. A sheepdog is a problem-solver. It calculates and strategizes with traits built on a foundational unit. This noble creature possesses genuinely heroic tendencies and is active, intelligent, instinctual, tireless, brave, and focused when it comes to the management of its flock. It lives for the challenge. In human form, sheepdogs make the tough calls, protect the team, and are instrumental in growing the herd (or business). If you want to hire a manager, look for the sheepdog types.

Then there are wolves. This species has its own place in the ecosystem (or workplace). Wolves are also strategic and loyal to their own pack and self-interests. These magnificent creatures get things done, that's for sure. They are adrenaline-fueled predators, taking what they want and feasting. Look at them as the human embodiment of the dopamine response and imagine them on your sales team. Yes, the prey-driven wolf goes beast mode in an environment that requires them to hunt (or bring in the deals).

Since symbiotic work environments involve all three personality types, which resonates with you? Which embodies who you are? Where do you fit in the business ecosystem? How best can you use your talents? Or...are you something different? Below we discuss another role that might supersede everything discussed in the management hierarchy.

The Shepherd

Notice that Chris Kyle didn't mention the shepherd in his quote. In my opinion, that's the role of a CEO and business owner. Entrepreneurs oversee the big picture comprised of the sheep, wolves, and sheepdogs who populate our teams. In my practice, it falls on me to handle internal and external threats with the appropriate human assets in place. That's what it means to be a leader.

Entrepreneurial success is not driven by a talent for getting things done through others. It also involves a hunger for winning and a thirst for knowledge.

Be the doer. Find motivation from within yourself. Feed your desire to win. Pursue knowledge that will allow you to achieve. The more productive input you allow yourself, the more productive output will come about. Create the life you envision. Make that life yourself while shepherding your team to the heights of success.

My next point is not a dictating theory, but rather the hard truth of reality. Approximately 1% of the world's population is considered wealthy. The number will not expand greatly, as it is a revolving door. Old money will die out, and new money will roll in. So, it baffles me that every day we hear "sheeple" saying, "Why does the top 1% get all the breaks?" It's because 99% of the world doesn't have the wherewithal to step outside the "comfort zone" and achieve—like the sheepdog, shepherd, and in some instances, the wolf.

Let's look at it in terms of "sheep power." A sheep will give you the power of a single sheep, never aspiring to the 1%. That leaves you, plus a one-sheep-powered business.

A sheepdog is significantly stronger and will give you exponentially more sheep power because its mission is to safeguard and grow the herd. Sheepdogs are natural team members and team builders. They intrinsically know the importance of loyalty and determination toward a goal, which allows for sustainability at the top.

Add some wolves that aggressively hunt prospects and land sales. They are innately gifted for the chase. Sure, you might experience a revolving door because wolves tend to go elsewhere when the pickings seem easier. Or they surround themselves with sheep or those of their kind in an attempt to rebel and lead the group, usurping the sheepdog's role, and challenging the shepherd. Therefore, they are apt to fall out of the 1%.

But by understanding the nature of the hiring pool, and with the right human assets in place, you can successfully develop a hybrid herd/pack that operates together as an alpha unit and lays it all on the line for the success of your enterprise. This type of unit will overpower competitors and has the potential to lead the industry.

Yes, success is truly all about your mindset and ability to lead. What type of mindset do you have? A millionaire's mindset, a winner's mindset, an entrepreneur's mindset? You have to be hungry with an insatiable and unquenchable determination to overcome obstacles and hit those goals, surrounded by the right team. You have to have the work habits and "coachability" of the sheep, the fearless prowess of the wolf, the loyalty and leadership of the sheepdog, and the visionary talents of the shepherd.

So, as the shepherd/CEO, you make your own breaks! No one is going to do it for you, ever. Privileged. Lucky. Narcissistic. Entitled. These are just a few synonyms that a loser will use to describe a winner. I hate to use the word "loser," but if you're blaming others for your inadequacies, then that's precisely what is happening—you're losing.

The Money Maker

As a winner, you never blame. You make your life what you want it to be. You make money where you want to make money, not where you have to make money. You can be driven by money but aren't reliant on it.

Those who are reliant on money need it. Those who are driven by money want it. If you need it, then you tend to focus more from a negative or desperate point of view. You have to be driven. With me, it's not necessarily the money that drives me but rather the satisfaction of reaching my goals. Remember I said earlier that when you focus solely on money and not the enrichment of life, the money becomes scarce. If you're doing the work for the money and not for passion you're missing out on a quality of life that is more important than monetary value.

Winners anticipate, and losers react. Those who choose to victimize themselves create false illusions. For instance, anyone who believes that sheepdogs and sheep are equals, despite the fact that sheepdogs do the heavy lifting, are dead wrong. No, sheep and sheepdogs aren't on an even par, not even close. Distinct attributes place the sheepdog on the opposite end of the spectrum. When sheep make excuses for their shortcomings, it's because they are too lazy, unmotivated, or ill-equipped to be the sheepdog.

The 99% will also say things like, "All you care about is money."

Who doesn't like money? If someone offered you the exact same job for $10/hour or $20/hour, which one are you going to choose?

Exactly, because you like money. The thing is, I will always get more excited about reaching my goals than the actual dollar amount. Sure, some of my goals are indeed monetary goals. I set these amounts to get myself where I want to go, but the true satisfaction is accomplishing what I set out to do.

When I was first starting out, I discussed with my circle of friends and colleagues my plans for the future, many ventures in different trades, and they looked at me as if I was crazy. They just couldn't comprehend how one person could pursue so many different things and have so many goals. They assumed my business opportunities were whimsical ideas that had no real way of coming to fruition. Elon Musk says, "Good ideas are always crazy until they no longer are." This just means the sheep do not share the same vision as the shepherd, nor the abilities of the sheepdog, nor the attributes of the wolf. To some, my ideas are whimsical because in their world, they simply aren't possible. In the shepherd's world, it's just another mountain on which to put his sheep.

People also question why I constantly fantasize about success. It's no fantasy. I call it being driven by success. Shepherds and sheepdogs are successful because empires rise or fall based on their passion and performance. It is simply a point of view. I am talking about getting out there and doing you. You kill it! Do you want to feast, or do you want famine? Feasting does not mean that you're "wolfing" down the sheep to get to where you want to go. Feasting means you're utilizing your sheep and sheepdogs (and in a limited capacity, the wolves) to allow all to feast.

The Seven P's

If you continue a cycle of mediocre rinse and repeat, don't expect an extravagant new outcome. Execution is the name of the game. You may have heard of the "Seven Ps," a British Army adage: "Proper Planning and Preparation Prevents Piss Poor Performance." Could there be better words to live by? I think not, especially when there are goals to hit and exceed. This is what being the Successor means in a nutshell. The initial blueprint for thoughtful, strategic, and opportunity-based decision-making hits the target and propels us forward. If this isn't already a generational philosophy passed down on your family tree and your business lineage, then start now. Expose your colleagues, children, and their children to the "Seven P's" and make that a part of your legacy.

Children are very insightful and will more easily decipher between failure and a problem that needs a solution. They can be shaped into problem solvers early on. Explain to them that those who embrace this notion will naturally rise above their peers. Talk the talk, walk the walk, and your kids will excel. It will spare them from morphing into people who cannot be productive without some authoritative guidance and ongoing babysitting.

Finding the Wins in Your Losses

There will be days when solving life's problems is harder than others. I call them "Rubik's Cube" days. We must understand that this is just part of life and business.

Do you think the sheepdog gets down on himself for not safeguarding a particular sheep from a wolf? Hell, yes! But he resets his vision, adjusts his game plan, and looks ahead to the next attempt, better prepared. You cannot be afraid of failing. Failure is a part of life and a part of business. **You have to find the wins in your losses.**

This is what I mean by finding a win in your losses. The only class that I failed during my doctorate program was biochemistry. I was required to take some general and organic chemistry prerequisites to prepare myself for the first trimester. It didn't help in the slightest! Being a nontraditional student, seven years removed from a classroom, I simply was not enabling the best habits to carry me through the program. Worse, I had no idea what my professor, Dr. Bracho, was talking about.

Dr. Bracho was a Venezuelan replica of Mr. Myagi. He had a reputation for being very challenging, so difficult that there were "I Survived Bracho" shirts for sale in the school's bookstore. The first three trimesters of the curriculum (the first four for me) had a Bracho class staring students in the face—biochemistry 1, biochemistry 2, and nutrition.

Like many current school curriculums, instructors teach to prepare students for standardized tests. As doctors, we were required to pass part one of the National Board Exams for admittance into the clinic and eventually the professional world as licensed doctors. Dr. Bracho's exams were geared very much to the process, and he wanted us to know the "why" in how certain components made the process work or why he was asking certain questions.

After failing my first round of biochemistry, I regrouped and surrounded myself with people who removed some of the friction of learning the process and getting through the class. During this prerequisite time, I befriended a guy in my class named Derek Douglas. Derek was, for lack of a better word, a genius. He was also a little older than our classmates; however, his delay in attending doctorate school was from military time rather than my Miller Lite time. Derek was also married with children, so we had something extra in common. Although we were in the same class, he required another trimester of prerequisites before getting into the program.

During my second attempt at biochemistry, I walked into the classroom to find Derek sitting front and center in the stadium seating that was Dr. Bracho's domain. That's precisely where I sat in my first attempt at the class, vigorously writing notes onto my printed-out PowerPoint slides. I figured this time around I would try the back of the classroom. I had already taken notes on all the material during my first failed attempt, so I was able to sit and listen. Surely, I would be able to pick this up.

Nope, Greek! Well, Venezuelan. As the first round of exams approached, I was fumbling through study guides and trying to make sense of the process. Once again, nothing was clicking for me. I knew Derek had a family and was also working at the local hospital, so I didn't want to bother him too much, but I was desperate. I called him up and asked if we could get together to look over the material. The test was first thing the next morning and he was working that night at the hospital. Still, he agreed to meet me in the cafeteria of the hospital on his lunch break to go over the material.

One hour in a hospital cafeteria changed my entire approach about how I was going to study for this class. Derek said things like, "If he asks this, he is looking for this," or "If this part of the process does not occur, what will happen?" Dr. Bracho allowed us to keep our exams after submitting our scantrons on our way out of the classroom. He reused most of the questions but changed one or two words and/or answer choices. Not only was I beginning to learn the processes of glycolysis and the Kreb cycle, but I was also learning Bracho's process.

He wanted us to zone in on a keyword and make the association to the correct answer, as did the boards. Each process was taught individually but are all connected in the body. Derek took all of the processes and drew them out in a chain linked display, and now, finally, it was making sense.

I didn't let the initial setback of failing the class deter my success. I simply had to learn what would work to facilitate that success. Although my first attempt at the course was definitely a disappointing rough patch in my academic career, I walked into the exam the next morning more confident than I had ever been entering a Bracho test. When the exam was handed out, I began my descent down the front page, "Keyword? Check! Associated word? Check!" By no means did I get an A, but I easily passed, and that's what I was looking for. Just get me to the next level.

If you're currently going through a rough patch, please don't let it discourage you. Let life's rough patches empower you, ultimately fueling your next move. After successfully passing the class the second time, I experienced no more setbacks. I found my groove in the system and went into each course and each exam confidently and decisively.

CHAPTER 7
YOUR PERSPECTIVE IS YOUR OBJECTIVE

Your perspective will either become your prison or your passport. It will either confine you to the way things are or launch you into the way things are meant to be.
~ Steven Furtick

When I first started this chapter, it was called "Put it in Perspective." Short, simple, and straight to the point, but then I got to thinking. Your perspective drives you throughout life. Life is a goal-driven journey that requires an objective. Your perspective is your objective! What are you trying to achieve in this life? We'll move through life, and superficial objectives will come and go, but our overall goal remains a constant.

I was filming a social media video the other day, and while editing, I thought to myself, *Man, my stomach is not as flat as it used to be*. Then I sat back and thought about the way my life is now. What is the point of having a six-pack anymore? It was nice while it lasted, but that is no longer my objective. For work, I frequently attend networking events with free drinks and hors d'oeuvres. Attending these events keeps me in the loop with other leaders in my community and in my industry. I don't want to stress out or get down on myself because I indulge at these events, enjoy a happy hour to relax or eat hot dogs and hamburgers with the kids. That is my happy place now. That is my new objective in my journey. My goal is to be successful in business and happy in my family life.

You should not be so in tune with one aspect of your life that you miss the music playing around you, because those things matter. Those things are what drive you to be your best, but what is your best? You must put your "best" into perspective. A crucial part of being successful is being able to put your life and your goals in perspective; being able to balance out the things that matter versus the things that don't hold much weight.

Remember the "work harder, not smarter" mantra that was my father's? As he is getting older, his perspective has now shifted, and he is realizing that working smarter is inevitably the correct choice. This was my vision from the very beginning. When my father asked me what my goals were financially, I responded with, "To make enough money to not have to do the things that I don't want to do." He looked at me and in an "I'm older and wiser than you" kind of look, he said, "That's not realistic!" That's fine. That's his perspective, but that is not me.

My paternal grandfather was a sun up until sundown worker, and my father is exactly the same. When I say worker, I mean physically working. I am currently in my early forties, and already, there are mornings when I wake up and feel every bit of sixty when I step out of bed. I can only imagine what I will feel like when I actually get there. Aside from the physical aspect of it, I want time to *work* on the business, building the brand and expanding to new business ventures. I want to do it comfortably and with minimal distractions.

We get to a point in our lives and our careers when tasks like maintenance on the car, mowing the lawn, deep cleaning the house daily, or cooking a three-course meal for dinner each night is no longer necessary, but rather distracting from our goals. To say that this thought is unrealistic is absurd. If it was indeed so unrealistic, then why do jobs for these tasks exist?

Housekeepers, mechanics, lawn maintenance companies, tax accountants and personal chefs are all hired daily to accommodate those of us who see their time as more valuable than the cost of these tasks. Fast forwarding to the present, I no longer mow or maintenance my yard, I no longer change my oil, I don't clean my house, I don't clean my pool, and I sure as Hell don't do my taxes. These are things that I don't want to do. There are still a few disgruntling items that remain on the list, but the time will come when those are marked off as well. All of these businesses are around for a reason. It's to provide a service for those of us who have the perspective to cut these mundane events from our lives and focus on reaching our goals.

Making substantial money is all about peace of mind, something you don't get from materialistic garbage. I'm not saying that you can't purchase nice things, but definitely not at the expense of your mental clarity. Those who choose to enjoy the lifestyle working in one of these professions do just that, enjoy it. That is their perspective, and I respect every aspect of it. I am writing this from an entrepreneurial point of view and emphasizing that we must play the cards that win us the pot.

It is imperative that we don't focus on the wrong aspects of business or opportunities that present themselves in life, for that matter. We need to recognize these opportunities—thoughtfully retooling our businesses, bolstering our knowledge, and supporting our communities—when they present themselves. There are fewer life-altering options that come into our lives than there are stagnant ones.

To give you an idea of how I viewed my time in doctorate school, I will give you a little background. I told you in the introduction that I was never much for attending school. I was kicked out of undergrad and then dropped out the next semester, only to re-enroll and finish a few years later. Not a lot had changed in my pursuit of becoming a doctor. I had a six to seven-year gap between completing my bachelor's degree and beginning doctorate school.

In the years between, I worked for a few gyms and owned my own personal training business. I went into doctorate school with more business knowledge than anyone else in my class. I was definitely not the smartest in my class, but I didn't let that deter me from being the best in my class. I simply applied effort where I felt effort was due. I was considerably older than most of the "kids" in my class, not to mention I owned a business, was married, and at the time had four children to tend to. When my classmates were up all hours of the night studying biochemistry, I was changing diapers and rocking kids to sleep.

I, myself, didn't get a lot of sleep, but I had a system in place, and I made it through. I was known as the guy who sat in the back of the classroom, only looked up from my phone or computer a few times each class and provided minimal engagement during discussions. I usually only studied for a few hours the night before exams and was content with receiving Bs and Cs. The point of this chapter is not to tell you that grades don't matter. In some instances, they absolutely do. Your GPA will really only matter in certain fields, such as acceptance into a number of programs or groups and boasting on your resume (not mine). But from a practical standpoint, those Bs and Cs got me to my goal, and at no point did I consider quitting before I got there.

The reality is, when you're in business, how many people will walk into your office and ask, "Excuse me, I am trying to find a new doctor. What was your GPA in school?" I knew what the requirements were to get through the program, and I met them, period.

We had a few people in my class who would literally throw a fit if they didn't get an A on an exam or the highest grade in the class. There were times when they sabotaged the study guides by changing just a few of the answers to assure themselves a higher grade (the study guides were in Dropbox as part of testing accommodations). As I coasted my way through the basic science courses and passed the first round of boards, I was eligible to enter our student clinic.

In the student clinic we treated our peers. I remember the day when incoming new students had orientation, and all those who were just starting student clinic swooped in like vultures trying to prey on the fresh meat in an attempt to acquire new patients. Once we had met the criteria to be checked out of the student clinic, we could move on to the outpatient clinic, which was a full functional clinic, on site at the school. There we had to go out in the community to find potential patients, and this was my time to shine! I breezed through the student clinic, but not before having all my ducks in a row for my transition to the outpatient clinic. Owning my own personal training business definitely gave me the upper hand on access to potential patients. I flew through the outpatient clinic, finishing my numbers faster than about 75% of the class ahead of me.

Midway through our clinics, my classmates looked at me like, *where did this guy come from?* No one expected the guy who sat in the back of the classroom and pulled the mediocre grades to just "get through" the program.

Was it because I was smarter than my peers? No! It was that I put into perspective what was important to my education. Did I want to thrive academically, or did I want to succeed in business? I chose to focus on the most applicable component of school. I took what I needed from the lectures and put it in my back pocket for the real world and I essentially memorized the rest of the material the night before the exam and brain-dumped it as soon as I was finished with the exam.

One of the women in my class, we'll call her Becky, was one of the aforementioned that had altered documents to have the highest grade in the class. Her perspective was, "If I make the highest grade in the class, then I will be the best doctor." I looked at learning much like this Mark Twain quote. It is said that Twain stated, "I have never let schooling interfere with my education." The majority of your education will take place out of the confinement of school walls or a textbook. Learning is done in the field, from experiences and interactions.

Becky did not have this. What she knew about the human body simply came from a book. Chiropractic is a field where you're in tune with the body and you know how it works on all levels. There is a difference between writing down the correct answer on a piece of paper and living the lifestyle that you preach about. If you sit down and think about it, those people that obsess over their grades are typically the ones that require a structured job. Entrepreneurs make their own structure that runs at their own pace. You must live what you sell, otherwise people will see right through it. It is a passion! Becky did not live her passion and she struggled as she got into a clinic setting. She could not bring in new patients, she could not communicate with established patients, she could not maintain a consistent schedule, and was simply unable to maintain her own structure to allow herself to be successful.

Becky began making excuses that required modifications by the clinicians, providing her with special treatment and limiting her time in the clinic. She did not realize that she would not be getting these same accommodations beyond the controlled environment in which the school's clinic provided. In the outside world, there are no special accommodations that help you achieve success. You either bust ass or look like an ass. I have used myself and Becky as examples to younger colleagues in my field, as well as stalling entrepreneurs.

I say, "Imagine Becky and I have offices directly across the hall from one another. Down this long hallway walks in a potential new patient. As the patient approaches, they see Becky and I both standing in the doorway of our practices. This patient does not know how we practice, what our GPA was or how fast we made it through clinicals. They know nothing other than what we look like and that we are doctors! They look at Becky, who obviously does not take care of herself and presents herself in a self-conscious manner. She is passive and does not make eye contact.

I, on the other hand, stand assertive and strong. I show confidence in my performance, and it is apparent that I practice what I preach. Now, which office is that patient going to walk into? The patient will come to me 95 times out of 100. People want to be inspired. She can be the smartest person in the world, but if she cannot relay that to her patients, then she will not maintain a successful practice. Her vast intelligence, in this case, is superseded by my ability to utilize mine.

Once business started to pick up, I began to lose focus on some of the other things in my life that were important. Quality time with my family, my health and fitness, and general maintenance around the house really took a backseat to the growth of my business. I acquired tunnel vision, losing sight of some things which made me the person I am today. Tunnel vision is good when it is productive and pushes you toward your goal, but not at the expense of the things and the people you love.

I often consult with my long-time friend Trent, who owns Aeromass Glass in Austin, Texas, about the progression of our businesses. To put it in perspective, when I opened my first practice, I was consumed with repaying loans for my initial capital, business loans for my operating capital, and managing payroll. I felt like every time I turned around, someone had their hand out, reaching for more money. I was becoming overwhelmed and had to sit down and prioritize who gets paid first. It wasn't to say that one creditor was more important than the other, but I had to look at it like, "Okay! Who will shut me down if I don't pay them?"

It felt like an endless cycle of disappointment. For a while, concluding every month, I told myself, *Okay, just keep the account over four figures.* This was where my perceived zero balance was at the time. If it dipped below that, I would begin to panic as a number of my bills were four-figure bills. In year two, I turned a corner, and I told myself to keep it above five figures at the end of each month. Before long, I did the same thing with six figures and eventually seven.

This is not saying what I make per month, but rather my new zero balance that we discussed a while back. It is simply a matter of how we view our situation. At this juncture, I could never imagine falling back below four or even five figures. However, at the time, that was my reality. I just had to make my reality grow.

One day, Trent and I had a conversation about the growth of our businesses. He was in his sixth year of business, whereas I was in my second year of practice at ProActive. As stated earlier, I dabbled as an associate to test the waters for a while before venturing out, but after running previous successful businesses, I decided it was not for me. Trent also started out with another company to learn the ropes before starting his own business. After six years, he was killing it. Our conversation went as follows:

> **Me:** Dude, I am currently at 78% of what I grossed all of last year, and we're not even through June.
>
> **Trent:** See? Boom!
>
> **Me:** I'm projecting a 57-60% increase this year. I'll guess the same, if not closer to 70% next year since I'll be hiring an associate.
>
> **Trent:** Nice, man! This past year was my first year going backward.
>
> **Me:** Hey, all businesses have that roller coaster effect. You just want to be the giant coaster and not a ride in the kiddie park.
>
> **Trent:** Yep.
>
> **Me:** Many years ahead of us.
>
> **Trent:** Yep. Mo money, mo problems.
>
> **Me:** More money, more responsibilities. All about how you manage them.

Then the conversation veered into trash-talking and mama jokes that are too explicit for this book, but this was a good representation of how to view progress. **If success was a continuous upward climb without any dips, no one would appreciate the sense of accomplishment.** We closed out the year with a 78% increase, and the following year even better. And we put our businesses in perspective—there won't always be an upward growth trend.

Look at 2020 for example, with Covid ravaging many businesses, either causing a revenue dip or even putting them out of business.

That's the challenging part of an upward trajectory. It plummets sometimes. The climb will stairstep, or as in this example, roller coaster, from one day to the next. We'll all have dips in our journey, but it's crucial that you regain momentum to shoot you back up to the next peak.

How Are You Filling Your Buckets?

Let's close this chapter with some productive imagery. Imagine your life as a giant balance beam. The beginning of your beam is where you are now. The end of your balance beam represents the end of your life. You walk across your timeline with a long balancing pole extending out in each direction from across your shoulders. Empty buckets are attached to either end of the pole. Whatever you decide to put into these buckets has to maintain balance as you walk through life. You may shift things around, but there must always be a perfect balance. See how the analogy works? If the two biggest priorities in your life are family and business, then put them in each bucket. These are your goals—a successful business and a happy family—and they hold a lot of weight. The greater the goal, the heavier the weight. Smaller goals that are less significant may add to a bucket, but again must be balanced out in your walk across the balance beam.

As you chip away at these goals, one milestone at a time, your balance might become skewed. So sprinkle in the less important things, like your gym gains, and get rid of vices to maintain your balance. You don't need the additional weight of alcohol, smoking, drugs, or sex mucking things up. The financial, physical, and emotional weight is enough to balance without these detriments.

The analogy is very similar to that of the highway example from *The Dopamine Response*, except that example demonstrated impulsive decisions that can lead you astray. This example pertains more to which areas of your life you are giving attention to. How you choose to fill your buckets determines your perspective of your journey.

I know this from firsthand experience. I've definitely encountered some setbacks in my life and overflowed my buckets with numerous vices. They sloshed with alcohol and bad relationships, and my body crumbled beneath the weight. There were several nights that I don't remember that preceded me waking up in a jail cell. It is what it is. This meant I spent a fair amount of my life playing catch up. I can't change it. I can only learn from it. The time in my life was a long, shaky and extremely dark walk across that beam, but it taught me more about myself than any other phase in life. It taught me that those things happened because I was filling my buckets with useless and nonproductive shit. As a testament to overcoming such adversity, I am proof that you can lay at rock bottom and still stand up and refuse to fail. You can reset and rebalance. You can correct a downward spiral. You can repair a destructive environment. You can come out on the other side.

Let's look at it this way. Harley Finkelstein, president of Shopify, says, "If you broke a lot of rules as a kid, you'd probably make a great entrepreneur." Many entrepreneurs have a specific wiring that leads them to be more susceptible to testing the waters. It's almost like it's ingrained in our DNA. Sometimes the water can get deep. Sometimes it can get rough. And sometimes you can drown. But you can always outshine your past if you choose to do so. You can always shift things from one bucket to the next—in my case, graduate school and a doctorate. Upon graduation, I replaced that weight of my buckets with new goals, such as starting a business and learning the finer points of investing. You, and only you, can maintain your balance. Life is worth the balancing act when the things you love exist in those buckets.

CHAPTER 8
BEING "PASSIVE"

He who works all day, has no time to make money.
~ John Rockefeller

This chapter examines the word "passive" from several different angles—the benefits of passive income, the restrictions we face when operating predominantly with an active form of income, and the proactivity we must undertake to bolster our mental health through setting up multiple passive money streams (peace of mind).

Passive income is the key that unlocks our financial success. If you do not have things set up to make money without physically working, then you have limited your success. You should be making money in your sleep. As silly or cliché as this may sound, I mean this in every literal sense of the term.

There are only so many hours in the day you can physically put in work and even fewer hours in the day that you can put in efficient work at an optimal level. Here's an interesting fact, though. Everyone has the same number of hours in the day. It's how you utilize these hours that makes you successful. Being an entrepreneur is hard work! Being a successful entrepreneur is even harder work. When you start out in a new business venture, it is a sun up to sun down, never turning off the brain, pride-swallowing, and ass-kissing venture. If you cannot handle occasional defeat, then this is not for you.

Passivity Vs. Activity

Let's break down the differences between passive and active income and give a few examples. An active income is your typical job. You show up and you do the work. If you make a certain wage, salary, or commission, then these are forms of active income. You're performing a designated duty that gets you paid an allotted amount that is congruent to the amount of energy that you put into that particular task or the amount of education that it took you to get there.

Active income is what we use to grow our equitable growth in order to invest in passive income streams to help accelerate our overall net worth. In the first seven years of being in practice, I was able to build the business close to seven figures. The early years of the chiropractic business were spent clawing my way through the trenches of actively earning, putting systems in place, learning what works, learning what doesn't work, and building awareness for my brand. The years went by, and we (I say we because it was a team effort with my wife and staff) streamlined a process that turned us into a self-sufficient, well-oiled machine. There was only one problem—I was still actively in the office, when I would much rather be working on investment deals with Kathy, vacationing with the family or playing a round of golf with the guys.

Let's imagine my current investment journey as a multilane highway (love those highway analogies). Each lane of the highway represents another money stream. In the beginning, I started my practice as a beaten down, rusted, stick shift truck driving down an old back road, kicking up dust. It was slow and it was bumpy, but it got me down the road with a lot of work. As I cruised along this road, I was able to upgrade to a newer vehicle and the road became paved. Still, I was the one actively driving. As I began to invest in more and more passive projects, my road began to widen into a beautiful, multilane highway. Each investment represents its own lane and should not merge with another. As we take our equitable growth that we have saved up through other investments, we may create a temporary bottleneck in the lane to construct the new investment's lane. Once this is completed and flowing with mass amounts of traffic (cash flow and equitable growth), you'll see rapid growth to your net worth. This process will continue until you have reached your destination.

I plan for my future and visualize the infrastructure needed to allow travel on my highway or highways. I reference my investment timeline with the franchising of my practice, plentiful real estate ventures, and the number of "whimsical" aspirations I have planned. The more lanes that I have flowing freely on my highway equals the level of success in which I can achieve.

You can also look at your multiple money streams as the widening of "the highway." When we have a single-lane road, there is a limited amount of traffic—or money, for example—that you can flow through. As we start to grow these money streams, we begin to widen our highways to allow more traffic to flow "seamlessly" without interruption.

What causes highways to widen? The growth around it. What causes the growth around the highway? A greater flow of traffic.

Rewinding back a few years, I will show you how I added lanes to my highway. Year after year in the office, our patient base and revenue continued to grow. Moving into year five, it was now time for me to start implementing some passive income strategies to snowball my income. In 2019, my wife and I purchased a few acres on the outskirts of Bryan, Texas, where we planned to build our forever home. For months, we walked the land, surveying the layout of the house that we had already designed, and began clearing trees and brush from the property to allow ample space for our kids to play. Everything was falling into place until Covid…and BOOM. The price of building materials skyrocketed, putting the cost of building our dream house out of the realm of what I was willing to pay at the time.

After sitting back and evaluating, we decided to sell the land. We took the substantial profit that we made on the sale and transferred it to a condo on Lake Conroe. This was our first true passive income investment. We quickly furnished the condo and listed it on a number of short-term rental sites and began booking tenants. The initial goal was to cover the mortgage through rentals, gain more equitable growth through passive sources, and, lastly, have a place for our family to get away from time to time. For the next 18 months, while the rentals were picking up steam, I trained my associate to build him up and allow myself more free time to spend on outside endeavors.

Following this year-and-a-half window in early 2023, we purchased a long-term rental property near our family's home. Although the tenants requested a ten-year lease, which would have been great to secure a long-term passive income stream, we opted to go with a three-year lease. This allowed flexibility to alter the rent based on the market or sell the house to apply our gains in a more profitable venture. A mere three months later, we stumbled upon the opportunity to buy into a pre-existing gym franchise. We bought this fully staffed and operational business with the intent of bringing in yet another passive money stream. However, we quickly realized that we'd be investing some sweat equity for a period of time before we could enjoy the fruits of our labor.

At this point, I'm able to sit back and breathe, but still have that growth mindset of pushing myself to get exactly where I want to be. My primary source of income is the chiropractic practice, with an associate to bring in money when I'm not in the office and provide fuel for the next adventure. Three other sources of money are coming in and counting, and I'm currently negotiating the buyout of another local chiropractic office in the College Station area to diversify my portfolio. This office primarily deals with a specific niche in chiropractic care that I do not specialize in with the current office, providing the opportunity for me to ensure I'm not leaving any stones unturned. Just like the franchise, it is staffed, fully operational and immediately profitable.

I could easily work until I'm 60-65 years old, build up a hefty savings account, sell my practice for over a million, and live comfortably throughout my golden years. Remember the sell out formula back in *Brick by Brick?* There are many of us who, at retirement, want to wash our hands of the business, get our big pay out, and walk away, but what if we looked at things from a more passive lens?

Earlier we discussed formulas that will allow us to profit from selling our business and cashing in on all our hard work, but what if we could convert our active income to passive income as we transition into retirement. Let's say that you start a business. Initially, this is an active form of income. You put in the hours to make it operational, and you actively grow the business into a major enterprise. Along the way, you recruit a number of reliable sheepdogs who share your vision. Eventually you get to a place where it all runs itself and you've put the right pieces in place to step back. Each location or each branch of the operation will create another lane on that highway, expanding your map into a passive financial enterprise.

Over the past few years, I've strived to mentor new and upcoming doctors with the intention of franchising the ProActive brand. The model is set up to fund the conception of each and every location, appointing my new eager-to-succeed doctors as the franchise owners and subsequently collecting indefinite franchise royalties throughout my retirement. Rather than selling the business for a larger lump sum, which will likely run out, I have chosen to expand my model and provide lucrative jobs for each of my successors, all while receiving an indefinite supply of mailbox money.

Each of those successors would intently learn the process of the franchise throughout their tenure in the office. Early in their academic careers, we would plot a location for their future practice per their preference or hometown, the population and demographic of that location, and the location's accessibility. As their graduation approaches, we break ground to start the build or seek a lease in a pre-existing location. As mentioned, the goal is to create wealth for my successors as we simultaneously pad our retirement fund. I supply all initial capital that is needed to get the business up and running for the first three months. At that point, the appointed franchisee would begin repaying the loan, while being fully responsible for all operating costs. Until capital is repaid, a higher, but still modest, percentage of the location's revenue will be set as the monthly payment. At the time that the loan is fully repaid, the percentage will then drop to a lower percentage, which will be paid indefinitely, as payment for the order of operations, brand awareness and consulting from the owner.

Richard Branson says, "Train people well enough so that they can leave but treat them well enough that they don't want to." This is very true, but there is a missing variable to this quote. It's the desire to fulfill the dream. Just remember that no one is going to work harder for your dream than you. It is your job to open their eyes to the dream in order to passively facilitate your dream.

The point of sharing my entire current and future processes is to inspire others to do the same. Multiple passive money streams amplify success. I often say, "Chiro is my capital." I love what I do, but there are many bigger dreams that I want to fulfill, as I've explained. I have so much creativity seeping out of the constraints of my office. I'm always looking for more ventures and up for more challenges. True entrepreneurs have the need to continue to test themselves and dare themselves into new experiences. Idle hands and minds do not allow for the entrepreneur to have true fulfillment in singular ventures.

Having a finite retirement would still create the stress of budgeting throughout my long term when I would rather spend that time living my life as the passive income consistently rolls in.

The Passive Piggyback

As we discussed previously in *Brick by Brick,* our primary goal of the short-term phase is to grind hard and save as much money as we can. These savings supply capital for all future endeavors. When we invest ourselves in our business (or businesses), it is crucial that we are not initially spreading ourselves too thin, but rather filling the pot that will allow us to prosper through diversity down the road. If we begin our journey by taking on too much at once, we tend to really water down the product. Your product, your dream, whatever that may be, deserves your maximum attention. Your dream may be to have a chiropractic office, commercial real estate, write a book, own a restaurant, and whatever else. That is fine. Just not right out of the gate. Trying to initiate and maintain this juggling act will leave you running on creative and productive fumes. These balancing acts are tricky. Prioritizing is a must. Putting the endeavors first which will plant the seed for Will's "home run" investments is vital.

Look at it this way, you must become the king of one realm before you can be the jack of all trades. For me, that was the chiropractic office. It was a system in which I had perfected over time, and it allowed me the ability to eventually branch out into other fields. Impulsively putting the cart before the horse and dabbling halfheartedly in multiple projects will cause that one trade or trait that makes you attractive and unique to become diluted, thereby resulting in an underperforming version of your potential self.

By putting all of your efforts into being the King will then allow you to set up subsequent investments that will simply piggyback off of each other, one after the next. We continually snowball our efforts down the hill until momentum takes over and we begin growing at an exponentially rapid pace.

By piggybacking, I don't necessarily mean that each endeavor should be in the same field. It should just be able to feed its succeeding venture.

The question then becomes, *how do I know how to prioritize my endeavors? Will the area in which I can become King be enough to get me to the next entrepreneurial level?*

On a fall afternoon, I met with architect and serial entrepreneur Chris Lawrence at a local café in downtown Bryan, Texas. Chris is the often-mentioned godfather of downtown Bryan, enriching the area with numerous development projects that will provide modernization, culture and revenue while preserving the area's rich history.

It was a very casual conversation with both of us discussing current projects in the works and future projects in our vision. With a substantial head start against me in the investing game, Chris's projects were beyond anything on my current level. Always humble, he intently listened to my endeavors and ideas. I inquired about the growth and development of everything he was doing, taking mental notes of his process to allow myself to level up to that stature more quickly.

Project after project, Chris rattled off a list of things that he was currently working on and what was in store for our up-and-coming downtown area. I was amazed at the way he was able to keep everything straight and not become overwhelmed with the scheduling of everything, so I asked, "how do you juggle everything at once?"

His response was simply this, "I prioritize everything in my schedule. Anything currently in construction priorities takes precedence over development or other priorities and I make sure to prioritize my passion and creativity for the project above any monetary value."

Much of our conversation was an aggregate of those who have reached a level of financial stability, which allows an individual to invest in various projects and pertains more to the present scheduling process. It didn't focus as much on what it takes to get there and how to prioritize your life leading up to this point. When looking at things from a more entrepreneurial and global perspective, Chris further added, "Young entrepreneurs are a special case because they don't know what they don't know—and that is both a blessing and a curse. You don't want to stifle new ways of looking at problems/solutions with prescribed methods of achievement. At the same time, they often need a framework. The notion of priority first still works but its application might have some specific differences. For one, they must be somewhat selfish in the aspect of self-preservation and the prioritization of that. I see quite a few entrepreneurs failing because they simply failed to figure out how to make money and survive while focusing on their new efforts. It's one of the biggest struggles I see."

By strategically planning our endeavors to promote stronger present day-to-day operations and implementing the systems that we learned in *Brick by Brick*, we are further capable of achieving the entrepreneurial prioritization which was discussed between Chris and myself.

Mental Health

You're probably wondering why I'm including a subchapter on mental health in a passive income chapter. The reason is twofold. First of all, mental health is an often overlooked aspect of entrepreneurship that should absolutely be discussed somewhere in the book. Secondly, I placed it here to remind you that most passive income streams often originate as active endeavors. As we pile more and more onto our plate, often, it can become overwhelming. Mental disorders in the brain caused by chemical imbalances—bipolar disorder, depression, or addiction—are much more prevalent among entrepreneurs, often stifling their production and creativity. The ability to mentally handle the demands of such a diverse workload will decrease your levels of stress and your chances for burnout. I'm here to tell you that you cannot be consumed in the chaos.

When planning out your "passive timeline," each endeavor should be plotted out accordingly and executed like clockwork. All gears in the clock must be in sync for the clock to operate appropriately. No matter how big or small the operational gear is, each one must fall precisely into place and meet the set standards to keep things rolling in your business — and in your life. But there are times when we experience an avalanche of adversity and fall into a mental rut. Sometimes things feel like they spin completely out of our control. Maybe they do. Shit happens. Whether it's a market setback, an investment that requires more active participation than you anticipated, employee issues, family issues, or a global disaster, you cannot let that overcome your dream. At other times, issues are created within our own minds, causing our judgement to be clouded. Success is founded on the ability to maintain clarity in the midst of chaos. Passivity is the crystal ball that allows us to see through the clutter.

It's just a fact of life, and how we address these valid concerns is what makes us successful. If you're pushing to get to the next entrepreneurial level through active forms of income, then you'll no doubt experience mental fatigue.

I wanted to get a professional's opinion on such a touchy subject, so I reached out to a local mental health professional, Christopher Stockwell, on the matter. He explained, "When our brains become flooded with an abundance of stressful endeavors, our bodies become stuck in a sympathetic nervous pattern, our fight or flight response, often called a sympathetic freeze. At this point, we stop using our brain's prefrontal cortex (where the real thinking happens) and our brains signal our bodies to release cortisol (our stress hormone) and adrenaline to combat these 'threats,' or in this case, our stressful endeavors. Our body's physical response to the 'flooding' is to respond in a manner that is hyper-vigilant, with increased anxiety, paranoia, and an inability to focus. All of these traits are detrimental to your success and must be addressed. Failure to address this unhealthy response to stress will ultimately result in profound unhappiness, destroyed relationships, and a slew of harmful physical side effects and mental illnesses."

The topic of mental health is still stigmatized in today's society, which shouldn't be the case at all. It's probably the most important and most neglected topic worldwide, especially since people are juggling overwhelming lives in an already complicated existence. When you are purposely adding to your plate, it's crucial that you do so very strategically. Unless you are the elite of the elite, there tends to be a "keeping up with the Joneses" scenario in an entrepreneur's life. It's never a bad idea to pursue resources that help balance life and maintain our mental health. How will your life's full spectrum fall into place if you're operating under debilitating mental stress?

Our physical, mental and spiritual health are equally important in your ability to sustain long term success. Unaddressed mental pressure can create a landslide of burdens. It's important to see the warning signs of potential disaster or understand how to avoid being trapped beneath the weight of it. Mental instability and unclarity is beyond crushing. Distributing the "stress" through passive streams is an alleviating factor that clears up mental capacity which will, in turn, allow for more creativity and energy for other projects or simply peace of mind.

There are days when I walk into the office, and my assistant has a dozen clerical issues that I need to resolve before I can even begin my day — stupid, tedious tasks that deter me from doing what I would rather be doing. These are things that must be done to proceed forward, and there are days that I don't want to do them, but I don't have a choice. These things can get to me. In other words, you're not the only one in the world feeling overwhelmed or in despair. You are part of a collective of entrepreneurs who face the same issues. I have days that I will sit back in my office chair and not want to do anything, venting to my associate; days when I'm driving down the road, screaming at incompetent drivers; or days when I'm struggling to co-parent with my ex-wife and life feels hopeless. Once I get through the mental angst of the situation and stop feeling sorry for myself, I sit down and think, *What in the fuck do I have to be upset about?* I have an amazing life. I have a great career, a great family, houses, cars, and all the luxuries that I would ever want.

You may be thinking, *Of course, you don't have anything to be upset about. You're successful.* I am now, but only after pulling myself up by my bootstraps and getting the right help. I've been through numerous struggles that many other entrepreneurs face, from financial pressure to feeling like I needed to check myself into a mental institute due to an abundance of stressors hitting me all at once. I've referenced being homeless and sleeping on people's couches in my earlier years. It's a horrible feeling, no doubt. I've been fired from jobs and denied on job applications. Also sucks. We must learn how to overcome these situations. **Resistance must be met with resilience.** Our mentality determines our means of overcoming difficult situations.

When faced with overwhelming issues, one strategy is to write the problems in preparation for striking them off your list. One way to achieve this is to consider the guidance in this book. It's true I'm a chiropractor and not a psychiatrist, but mindset and mental states are huge parts of my message. Whatever hole you find yourself, whatever void you stumble into, and whatever obstacle that threatens your success can be overcome with self-discipline, super effort, therapy, and the stubbornness to hang in there until your list of problems is empty and the goal is met.

Throughout business, and life really, if not controlled, your mental health can really get away from you due to the copious amounts of stressors that are thrown in your face. It's a feeling that when even if everything in your life is moving in the right direction, you still feel like you're drowning. It's this feeling of panic as you frantically tread water. We seemingly put our foot on the accelerator to speed through each checkpoint until we've reached our final goal. During this time, it's not uncommon to put our blinders on to the journey—that beautiful journey—that deserves so much gratitude.

Ultimately, our abundance of passive money streams will allow for something more precious than money. It provides mindfulness. As we get to the point where we fully transition from active to passive earning, our ability to stop and smell the roses becomes abundant. Our stress levels diminish, our financial levels are steadily flowing, and our future endeavors are now optional. Up until this point, we have been mindful of every aspect that allowed us to get to this point. We have been consumed with every component that makes our life operational. Now that our money is working for us, we can be more mindful of the things and the ones that we love around us. Once you have achieved this level, you will have unlocked a whole new level of freedom in your life.

CHAPTER 9
YOUR INNER CIRCLE

Expand your inner circle to include those who can challenge your thinking and escalate you to unreached heights of success.

~ Simon T. Bailey

The previous chapter discusses the actual money streams that you set up for yourself, while your inner circle focuses more on those with whom you surround yourself and how those people affect your success. Note that each circle is important in the overall system and may overlap. This is important.

All of the talent, all of the hard work, and all of the discipline in the world will appear minuscule if you fail to build a network of like-minded people who share your vision.

I'm not the smartest guy on the planet. I'm a visionary. That's why my supporting cast is so important in enabling me to reach my goals. Those "inner circle" people can elevate your stock or tear you down, so it's essential to be selective. Who you let in makes an indelible mark on the group as a whole. Be vigilant about "energy vampires" and those who drain your battery. There must be reciprocity. What goes out must be replenished, and vice versa, in these special edifying friendships.

Each circle you put together will serve a specific purpose. Your numerous inner circles will interweave into a large network diagram, and you're the sole common entity amongst all. Some people or components may share common circles, but you're the epicenter that binds them together.

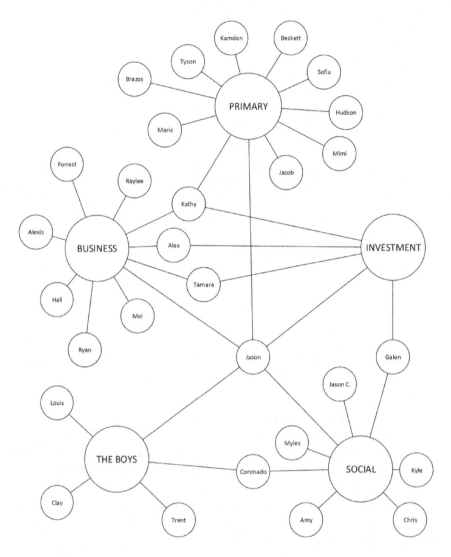

When we stop to look at our array of individually purposeful inner circles, not so much as a solar system with each circle trapped within the next, but as our universe, we see that each circle holds a different purpose. Each purpose may independently function as opposites but are all synergistic in achieving life's ultimate goal—success.

Darren Hardy says, "Along your heroic journey toward success, you will have setbacks. That is when it is most important to have the right people around you, to remind you that you can and will succeed."

Just because people aren't in your inner circle doesn't mean they can't influence your success. Their influences just manifest in different ways.

My circles are important components of my life that require support to thrive. My family circle is made up of my wife and kids. This circle is primary—it is the nucleus of everything that I am working for. Fulfillment of this circle breathes life into the remaining circles in my diagram. This circle feeds my will to strengthen my other circles, but then reciprocates the benefits of those surrounding circles. I have *The Boys,* which is basically a group thread of nonstop, immature bantering with my high school buddies who are spread out around the state. This circle is tightly woven with longstanding and strong relationships. My business or office circle consists of my doctors and staff. This circle allows me to grow in my business by carrying out responsibilities to keep the machine running. As the business expands, each location will have its own circle that fits within my universal business circle. My investment circle is comprised of like-minded investors and motivated entrepreneurs with similar visions who I can bounce investment ideas off and/or facilitate future endeavors. This circle is separate from my business circle, as this circle promotes more passive income. And my social circle has newer friends I spend time with on a day-to-day basis. These relationships provide me with my day-to-day interactions and friendships. This is the "cash flow" of my relationships and friendships that promotes daily accountability.

Each circle has a specific function to the overall balance in the ecosystem that is my life. There are a few overlaps, but I'm the common denominator and serve as the center of my network.

Most of my primary circle—(from left to right) Sofia, Kamdon, Tyson, Kathy, me, Brazos, Beckett, Hudson.

Maris aka Mare Bear (my favorite Care Bear).

Hudson showing off his medals from his jiujitsu tournament.

Kamdon and Sofia supporting their big brother, Tyson, with Texas Tech gear, while Maris looks on.

Drafting Your Team

Jim Rohn says, "You're the average of the five people you spend the most time with." They know where you want to go. When you're building your professional network, you must surround yourself with the people who will benefit you the most and do so by plugging in and making the team operate as a whole. You want to surround yourself with superstars, including your clients.

Say you're drafting your fantasy football team. You don't draft your bench first. At the same time, you don't draft a team solely of quarterbacks because you'll be leaving a lot of crucial, designated positions unattended. Instead, you strategically draft the best player on the board who will suit the operative needs of your team. The team is a machine, and everyone plays a role. It reminds me of my investment circle.

For example, in a recent project, four of us put our heads together—me, my wife Kathy, and another couple, Tamara and Alex. First, there's me, full of ideas and always wanting to press full steam ahead. Kathy is the detail chick who fine tooth combs our endeavors and often operates as CEO. Tamara is the marketing whiz who helps to amplify our success, and Alex is our voice of reason and seeks out any obstacles or conundrums that may occur.

Are the people you surround yourself with making your net worth rise or fall? These people share a vision with you—your vision! Your mission statement! How do you forge a thriving system? You have to break it down and see who fits in. Let's go back to sports for a moment. It's like an athlete who has an amazing year with a team, and then decides to chase a bigger contract or join a championship contender…and completely flops. Why do these superstars falter after just one year? They get plugged into a new system, and most of the time it's a system that doesn't work for the incoming superstar. Or the system isn't in need of the strengths that player brings to the table.

The contribution has to suit the system's needs. If you aren't a sports connoisseur, the same analogy applies to music as well. Most of the time, bands have spent years together, fine-tuning their style and brand. They're a well-oiled machine, bouncing ideas back and forth and crafting hits. Then one of the members thinks, *Why have a piece of the pie when I can have the whole thing to myself?* Egos get involved! Most of the time, it's the lead singer because he or she is the "face" of the band. So, just as the band achieves exponential success, all of a sudden, the face of the band comes down with a case of LSD (lead singer disease).

A band I loved growing up was Matchbox 20. When they first came out, they absolutely crushed it. Their sound was so "smooth" (a lead singer Rob Thomas reference), and the band was one of the top acts in their era. Eventually, Rob Thomas decided it was time to go solo. The band dissolved, and he had a few decent singles as a solo artist, but never matched the success that Matchbox 20 experienced.

Their system was torn apart, and Rob had to create a new system, which lacked the dynamics of the original band. Matchbox 20 was established with every band member having an equal respected vision. As a solo act, Thomas had a band for hire with revolving parts and only his vision.

As you'll read in the next chapter, consistency is one of *The 7 Cs* that makes one successful. There is no consistency in revolving doors. However, you do have anomalies like Justin Timberlake. Not to say he didn't put in the work and isn't extremely talented, but he's one of those rare cases that broke away from his original circle to experience exponential success. I don't have a *Whatever You Touch, Turns to Gold* chapter, but if I did, it would be one page and just have a picture of his face. So let's focus on a higher probability of success by drafting a team who are invested in the goal, put the team first and share your vision.

The Boys

This circle consists of a bunch of degenerates from high school who all broke the mold in the real world. These guys and I were just searching for something different in high school, and somehow, through a shitload of hard work, discipline, and effort, we all managed to become successful and thrive as adults. I don't want to use the word rejects when reminiscing, but we all steered away from the superficiality of the "in crowd," although my upbringing inherently pushed me in that direction.

As I was growing up, my family lived in a nicer neighborhood, I played travel baseball, my family spent a lot of time with the prominent families in our area, and I was groomed to be the preppy kid on campus. However, I somehow always gravitated back to my circle— *The Boys*. I preferred standing under the stairs outside in the high school courtyard playing hacky sack in our baggy jeans with wallet chains or spending Friday and Saturday nights as mallrats, causing mayhem in the local mall. Trent, Clay and I are the three members who have been there since the beginning.

Clay and I grew up across the street from each other as kids and were even kindergarten classmates. We spent many days playing baseball or football outside, riding bikes throughout the neighborhood and rushing to get home before the streetlights came on at dark. As time went on, Clay focused more heavily on baseball and subsequently was drawn towards his opportunity to excel in his athletic endeavors versus participating in the rest of our group's shenanigans. I met Trent and Lance in a middle school art class and for the next few years we were inseparable. We were a trio of mischief, creating crude cartoons of middle school humor, pranking our classmates and convincing our art teacher, Miss Beaulieu, to give us all hall passes for us to roam the halls of the school. Whether it was struggles at home or personal spats within our group, we went through many highs and lows together throughout our teenage lives. During our junior year of high school, we noticed Jeremy, a long-haired surfer kid, wearing a huge 90's style hemp necklace and Pennywise band t-shirt sitting alone at a table in the school cafeteria. We quickly made our way over to him and adopted him into our group. Our group was complete—the infamous J²LT. Following high school, Lance and Jeremy moved away and lost touch, but Trent and Clay have remained constant.

I left town after high school, and although there was a brief period of silence while I was in that little farm town in Missouri, we picked up right where we left off. In our twenties, we managed to add two more to our trio—Coronado and Louis. Coronado (nicknamed Cor-nerd-o by my kids) was a year older than us and joined the group years later. Louis's wife and Trent's wife were friends in high school and ironically discovered that both couples moved just two hours away, completely unaware. They ended up two streets away from each other. This completed our group.

With Coronado also living in the Bryan/College Station area, he double dips in my social circle of people whom I spend much of my time around. We are polar opposites of each other in the sense that I am very hard-nosed and assertive, and he is probably the most laid-back person I have ever met. It provides my daily life with great balance.

In the conception of ProActive Chiropractic, I was not in a position to fund my dream. Aside from the help I received from my family, Trent loaned me $5000 as part of the initial capital I needed to launch.

At this juncture in my life, I was completely broke, and $5000 was a lot of money. However, he was in a place where it didn't cause any hardships to loan it to me.

Remember the guys at the blackjack table? I couldn't believe it. Although it was a friend loaning me the money, I wanted to treat it as a business transaction, so I asked him, "What are the terms? When do you need it back, and what's the interest?"

After he had already wired me the money, he just said, "Man, there's no interest. Just don't take twenty years to pay me back." He didn't have to do it, but he knew that's what it would take to get me over the hump. It was a selfless act for the betterment of our circle, and I'm forever grateful for that. We all rely on one another for accountability to maintain the strength and integrity of our circle. At this juncture, we have very little professional crossover in our money streams, but that's not the purpose of our circle.

This group is an escape from reality and takes me back to a more carefree youth, giving us a chance to unwind for a minute. It's a healthy back-and -forth banter that provides some lightness to the day. We trash talk nonstop, enthusiastically root for the Houston Astros, and dog on Clay for being a Yankees fan, but we are all there for each other when it comes down to it.

Jeremy, Lance, me and Trent—Junior year of high school.

Louis, Trent, me and Coronado – following Game 6 of the 2022 World Series.

Jason C, me, Coronado, Trent and Clay – my wedding reception

My Office Circle

You must surround yourself with a team that makes you a better person and builds a better brand. When I first opened the office, I tried to oversee everyone—the front desk manager, the massage therapists, the billing company, everyone. This operating system was incredibly exhausting, and I was not able to work to my potential in the areas that I needed to focus on. My main areas at that time were the treatment of the patients and marketing outside the office. I began to lose sight of my vision because I was too busy trying to do everyone else's job on top of my own.

In other words, I was overly active in matters best left to my team. As the owner, I wanted to be assertive and establish my position. However, being assertive does not mean being up someone's ass 24 hours a day to make sure they get the job done correctly. If you're micromanaging your staff all day, every day, then you're consumed with duties preventing you from reaching your goals more efficiently. It was time for me to trust my office circle.

True, as an entrepreneur of a start-up, you'll be doing a lot of the initial grunt work. There are times when you'll have to coach a teammate or do some minimal micromanaging-type teaching on specific, important tasks, but this cannot be your overall business structure. You'll put in the hours and pay the dues to get yourself to a place where you can surround yourself with talent, which in turn allows you to shine brighter. When these individuals are brought in, train them properly and then let them do their job. You must create an environment that is going to accommodate your dreams.

With that being said, it was vital for me to establish a chain of command within my office circle, which would allow the business to grow. It was necessary to build this hierarchy in the office to promote greater communication between the assistants and the doctors, as well as delegate tasks to their appropriate department. I needed to bridge the gap between the hands-on and hands-off approach, later understanding this as allowing me to differentiate between active and passive duties.

From the beginning, the goal was to bring in a manager to act as a hub to the company, not just the initial location, and be the glue that binds each location together under the ProActive umbrella. For years we had been operating the front desk with multiple assistants who had come through. Their aspirations revolved around patient interaction and not admin work. This was when I found Alexis, who had been working for the gym I had recently bought and was looking for a bigger position with more responsibility. She arrived in the office on her first day eager to learn and showed immediate signs of leadership and problem-solving skills that led to great improvements of efficiency and communication in the office. The culture within the office began to take shape through training and collaboration. I communicated my immediate and future goals for the direction of the business, and she was able to help steer the practice in that direction. Filling this position allowed my practice to thrive in a way that it hadn't before. My focus was more on the patients and expansion of the business.

To reiterate, you're putting a ceiling on your success by micromanaging. Not only does micromanaging put a cap on your income, but it implies you're a poor judge of character and lack the ability to motivate others. You can only be in so many places at once, so delegate. List the most important business duties and tackle those responsibilities head-on. These are the things that the business absolutely cannot thrive without. The further my business circle progresses into the future, my position becomes more and more business oriented, allowing me to spend time building up my investment circle.

My Investment Circle

When I envisioned the investment group, I imagined Knights of the Round Table, where everyone has a vision and voice, but we all stay dialed into the same objective. This isn't a boardroom with one member barking orders or dominating the task at hand. It's a think tank and collective effort which yields the best results. Everyone has their role to ensure no overpowering voice distracts the group from the goal.

A while back, I had a patient by the name of Galen come into my office. He was very talkative, quirky and was obviously very well versed in the world of investments. I specifically remember a day early on in his treatment in the office when Galen was laying face up on the treatment table. I was providing soft tissue treatment on his neck when we struck up a conversation regarding the stock market. He began telling me about how he had been in the Air Force, then followed that up by training to be a pilot, before deciding to step back completely and solely invest in the market from the comfort of his own home. He knew the ins and outs of any investment that he chose to pursue. He would wake up in the morning, begin his research, analyze the trends and invest accordingly. His ability to use this as his sole source of income was very intriguing, especially considering it was a substantial income. At this point, I was relatively new in the market and was desperately seeking a mentor to show me the ropes. Galen stepped in as this mentor. He provided the core to my investment circle that allowed me to strategically build around.

Over the years, he would guide me through the volatility of the market and provide reassurance when things got hard. When the market was plummeting, he reminded me of one of his favorite quotes by Baron Rothschild: "The best time to buy is when there's blood in the streets, even if the blood is yours." When the market would begin soaring upwards and I would get that euphoric feeling of reaching the peak, he would remind me that just beyond that peak will follow anxiety and desperation when the market reveals I've overstayed my welcome. Beyond that, we began discussing various endeavors to chalk up more passive income streams, from vacation rentals to laundromats and various inventions. We often bounce ideas off each other, ask for each other's approval on certain projects or simply have general think tank ideas over a couple of beers.

His ideas over the past year have shifted more to product development, with him inventing the new Muddiez floating cooler, something that he had been imagining for years. We sat down one day and he explained to me his production process, his marketing campaign and his vision for where he wanted his new invention to go.

It's people like this who stir the pot to your creative brew. This is where you excel from good to great. It's surrounding yourself and filling your round table with similar creative minds.

At the end of the day, you must ask yourself regarding each of your circles, "What is my circle doing for me? Are the members discussing various business ideas, sharing like-minded successes, and encouraging potential investments? Are the members invested in you as a person, concerned about your wellbeing, and motivating you with constructive competition?"

These are examples of positive inner circles that provide support for your endeavors. What we don't need is a circle composed of gossip, constant bouts of the blame game, and sheepish (victim) mentalities. Those types of circles will get you nowhere. Think of people that you find inspirational, admirable, and that push you to do your best in every endeavor. Those are the people you want to surround yourself with, those are your inner circle.

My Social Circle

It takes a village! This is what a social circle consists of. It's the accountability of everyday relationships that pushes you to be continually better. It's the extra set of eyes on each other's children to deter them from unnecessary mistakes. They are gym partners, happy hour companions, trustworthy sounding boards, and those who provide daily interactions and nonjudgmental transparency. Just as our passive income streams, this circle provides us with daily doses of positive mental health. People in my life like Coronado, Jason C., Amy, Chris, Kyle, or Galen provide a constant reminder that I always have someone to lean on in a time of struggle or celebrate with during a time of achievement.

Another strong characteristic of this group is that it helps maintain positive direction through healthy habits and deter us from destructive patterns. This is enriching. A strong and caring support group will give you the hard truth when needed and a daily dose of reality. These relationships enrich your life consistently.

On the evening of September 28, 2013, I was sitting in my condo in Kansas City with my son, Brazos, and my ex-wife. At about 9 p.m., I received a phone call from my friend Cliff, who had been a big part of my social circle throughout my time in mid-Missouri. Cliffie was calling with the exciting news that his wife was in labor with his first child. He told me they were in route to a hospital in Columbia, which was about an hour east of him and about two and a half hours east of Kansas City. During our five-or-so-minute conversation, he told me that his parents opted not to come to the hospital that night and basically left him to go through it alone. I could tell over the phone that he was nervous, but I reassured him that everything would be all right and hung up the phone.

I sat back down in my recliner and got back to my show, before pausing it and telling my then wife, "I'm going to Columbia."

"Now?" she responded.

I knew I had to be there for Cliff. I got dressed, threw an extra pair of clothes in the car, picked up a large cup of coffee and a few cigars, and headed two and a half hours east to see my friend. When I arrived,

I was greeted with a big hug and ushered to the room where they were. We sat and chatted for a few hours as the nurses monitored her vitals and progression. When the time came for the delivery, I saw myself to the waiting room, grabbed another cup of coffee, and waited for hours. Following the birth, I returned to the room to see his new baby girl. When the nurses took her away to administer the routine tests for the new bundle of joy, Cliff and I made our way to the parking lot and lit up our stogies. We stood in a cloud of smoke, talking about how great it felt to be a dad and doing a little reminiscing. Cliff expressed his appreciation for making the trip to be with him. We finished our cigars and had one last hug, and I made my way back to Kansas City. I tell this story because it exemplifies what you do for your circle. On many occasions, the sacrifices and encouragement were reciprocated by Cliff.

Your social circle adapts to whatever phase of life you're currently in. Those who make up this circle often come and go, but heavily influence the direction of your life. For many years my social circle perpetuated a very fun, yet destructive lifestyle. As I mentioned, I worked as a bartender for much of my twenties. I had my group of friends that I ran with, mainly to the bar. My day consisted of waking up after noon, meeting up with the guys, hitting the gym for a couple of hours, going home to get cleaned up, and driving up to work at the bar around 6 p.m. until it closed. All the while, the guys hung out drinking, then cleaned up and found an after-party. They went to bed at sunrise, then repeated the routine. My circle was fun and provided a ton of memories, but it did nothing for my future.

That group of friends has come and gone. A few of us still keep in touch and inquire about others' lives but are all in different places than twenty years ago. Although there are times that I miss those simpler times, my current circle is more aligned with the productive direction that I want my life to go. Where it is very likely that many of the current members in my social circle will transition into long term relationships, I can only expect that circle to change in years to come.

Take Out the Trash

There are two main ways people view and attain success. The first are those who go out and make it happen. They put in the work, acknowledge the amount of sacrifice needed to reach their goals, and then execute. It's a circle that fires on all cylinders and presses on to accomplish what they set out to do.

Remember, iron sharpens iron. Surround yourself with these people who hone your skills, push you to be the best version of yourself, and continually motivate you to hit your goals. Your team should be celebrating the highs, reevaluating the lows, and achieving the goals as a unit.

On the flip side, there are those who deter the group from their goals in order to level the playing field. They "want" success but avoid the hard work it requires, making it unattainable due to their own lack of effort. Often, these toxic and miserable people attempt to knock you down to allow themselves to appear successful. When the negativity of a circle member begins to outweigh the positive contributions, it's time to let them go.

The trade-off is that removing toxic people prevents them from taking up space and blocking productivity. Replace them with top performers. Much like the sheepdogs that we discussed a while back, it's important to our success that we surround ourselves with high performers. Simply being in the presence of a high performer will increase your overall performance or productivity. On the contrary, being accompanied by an under achiever will lower the overall performance with underwhelming results. If you're surrounding yourself with inferior people in an attempt to appear more superior, then it's time to take a personal inventory of your self-confidence, which we will cover in a later chapter.

If you're fueled with anger and resentment due to a circle member's contribution, or lack thereof, it's time to reevaluate your association. If someone is sabotaging your dream, then you must cut them out of that dream. Removing someone from a particular circle does not mean they cannot contribute or associate in a different circle. It just means that their contributions were not beneficial to the original circle's objective. If someone is toxic to all circles, then it is time to release these people from your life so you can fill the space with other people or things that really matter. So, take out the trash. Productivity cannot withstand continuous drama. **Drama is merely a person's attempt to remain relevant.**

Though it may be difficult and cause you to hurt and cause hurt to others, you must make the decision to move forward. Removing someone from your life sucks, but it allows space in your circle for someone who is more compatible with this juncture of your life. It doesn't matter how rich, how successful, how dominant, or how powerful you are. You still must O.W.E.—Outwork Everyone! Be the grittiest motherfucker in the room. That doesn't mean that you abandon the "Work Smart" motto, it just means that you put 100% into every single thing that you do. There must be constant, positive progression by everyone. No one can step down and allow another to step up. Two positives make a positive. One positive and one negative or two negatives ultimately result in a negative. Keep moving forward.

One of my sons was having some trouble with his dopamine control recently, just as most twelve-year-old boys do. Oh, the accessibility of inappropriate material on the internet these days. When I was a twelve-year-old boy, I had to sit there and wait for the obnoxious AOL download to finish and hope that no one picked up the phone to interrupt the dial-up, just to see a pixelated picture of a woman. Those were the days.

We had to sit down and have a talk about the decisions he was making and the people he was surrounding himself with. I asked him if his friends at school were looking at these types of materials as well. He acknowledged they had. I explained the Rohn Theory to him, explaining it in a similar basketball analogy. I asked him to name the five friends he spends the most time with. Once he listed his roster, I told him to imagine he was the coach of a basketball team, and those five friends were his starting lineup. He nodded that he understood the example. I then asked him, "If those friends' actions in life represented their basketball abilities, how many championships would the team win?" He looked at me and without saying a word, his face said *We ain't winning shit.* I then followed up with, "Wouldn't you want a team that would win you the championship year after year?"

He agreed that it would be in his best interest to have better players on his team. It's these moments that make us really analyze who we are putting in our circles and who is, for lack of a better word, the trash we need to take out.

What happens if one of your teammates constantly merges into your lane and forces himself into the role of main character in the cast? The lack of group effort slows you down and reduces the overall speed of your team to a subpar level. If a player on your team becomes distracted from the goal, individually, this will elicit inadequate performance and scarce possibilities of any overall success. Toward the rest of the team, it will project negative energy that seemingly and abruptly slows your momentum and forces everyone to drive on top of one another.

If you find yourself with teammates like this, it's time to take out the trash. Eliminate those around you who bring down your net worth. We cannot continue to drive this way and get where we need to go. When you allow negative people to deplete your energy source, your vision becomes clouded. This is not even in a metaphorical sense of energy depletion but also physical exhaustion. Light the way for those around you with positivity but remember that some prefer to remain in the dark. When that becomes the case, cut them loose.

When our mind and body can no longer operate at an optimal level, production will significantly decline. We see it in both the Jordan and the highway examples, and a wresting example that may resonate with some readers. When I wrestled or trained MMA, I did not want a training partner I could beat day in and day out. How does that allow me to become better? I surrounded myself with a group of elite athletes who all had unique, supreme strengths, so I could elevate my performance level in each of those areas and better myself. Taking a beating every day was not fun, and believe me, I took plenty of beatings, but I would rather learn in practice than lose in competition.

This setting was controlled by the environment. I set myself up for success by plugging myself into an already thriving team. I was expected to step up and perform at their level, or I was just another jobber who would lose every day. The choice was mine.

On the other hand, starting your own business is a different story. Initially, you are the team! Do you thrive, or do you falter? Will you press forward and climb the ranks, or will you settle with mediocre complacency? It is all on you. You may surround yourself with a team, but you're the driving force that puts the team members on the same page. Channel your inner MJ.

We may delegate tasks, but at the end of the day, if the business tanks, the other members will leave for other pastures while you're left cleaning up the mess you allowed to happen. They will not pick up the pieces for you. There is no relying on someone else to pull the weight for you.

There is a difference between delegating and relying on someone else to keep you afloat. If you're relying on someone else for your own success, then that person will continue to grow, and you'll stagnate. If you rely on someone to get you by, then you're a parasite in need of a host to survive who lacks initiative. Delegation of a task within a project is simply being part of a team. It doesn't matter where you rank within the team, exhibiting parasitic properties is a detriment to the overall goal.

The team you try to organize around yourself will pick up on this. When I first started in practice, I had a revolving door of assistants and therapists who worked for me and couldn't keep anyone around. I explained to them that the practice was still in the infancy stage and I couldn't just pay myself out of business. While they nodded in "understanding," deep down, they were going all Jerry McGuire and screaming, "Show me the money!" After three or four employees, I had to look at myself. I knew that I could not pay more than I was currently paying, but how could I lead them differently? How could I change their mentality from "Do I get paid today?" to "How can I help this business grow?"

These two mentalities play deeply into *The Dopamine Response*. An employee who is motivated to work hard to grow the business will experience happiness and financial gains. As Gary Vee says, it's "legacy over currency." You, as the owner (remember the Shepherd, Sheep, Wolf, and Sheepdog analogy), must instill that mentality in your employees. Very few "employees" have that innate ability to drive with that kind of focus. Otherwise, they would be business owners. However, just because they aren't an owner doesn't mean that they cannot be a vital part of the dream. Growth is only inhibited by the team's lack of vision to cohesively get to the next level, but it's your responsibility as the owner to instill that vision. Allow them to grow within the company.

On the flip side, parameters must be put in place to encourage success, particularly on the amount of delegation that is occurring. There must be a balance. I mentioned previously in *Brick by Brick* that I know of a seven-figure earning businessperson who, at the end of the day, has nothing to show for his work. I have a close friend who has fallen victim to this scenario. We've sat down and discussed ways to bring her back into the positive.

You must not fall into the trap of over-delegating to avoid work, which is what she does. However, she is still constantly working to keep up. Parameters were not set, and employees, associates, and outsourcing were all depleting funds faster than they were coming in. This happens to business owners who have built up their brand and rely on their name to get by, very similar to the band breaking up. By over-delegating, you're telling your company that you're above the company. It becomes a dictatorship that creates a downward spiral. The whole point of becoming a business owner should be that you grow enough to allow yourself more time to live the life you want to live.

Your lifestyle must be dictated by your income, not the other way around. Otherwise, you'll be on a constant grind to keep up. Upon opening my first location, I had scheduled how long I wanted to work per week by what was occurring in the business. Side by side, I had two timelines (three, if you include the investment timeline) that correlated with each other.

One, we had the growth of the business. Benchmarks reading "hire new associate" or "open second location" spanned the timeline. Adjacent to that timeline was my physical contribution to the business, an active income timeline, so to speak. Starting off in practice, I worked five and a half days a week. I had colleagues right out of school open their practices four days a week. This did not fit my model because as my business progressed, I wanted to allow more time for passive income.

Directly correlating with the "hire new associate" entry, the other timeline read, "Cut back to five days per week." This allowed the new associate to gain some traction in the business, freed me up for that half a day and began to funnel in more passive income. The model was designed to have me as the head doctor, then to hire Associate A and Associate B. Associate A would be groomed to take over the next location while Associate B would be promoted to the Associate A position. This trend would continue, increasingly growing my passive income, incrementally decreasing my hands-on participation in the office, and creating a recurring, passive income that would carry me comfortably through retirement, not to mention allow my children the opportunity to join an already successful business and let them grow that through the next generation.

As much as I love my job, it is hands-on and it does wear on the body. Besides, I would much rather spend my time with my family, enjoying time on the golf course or searching for my next business endeavor. I am doing the things that I have to do, so I can do the things that I want to do, actually *live* my life!

The Bond of Your Circle

The integrity of our circles is only as strong as the bond which binds its members together. The relationships within the circles and the objectives of those circles are what allow them to flourish.

I was 19 years old sitting in my college dorm room, wrestling season had just ended, and I finally had the chance to sit down and watch the movie *Remember the Titans*. The players, segregated by color, faced the adversity of working together as a team. Throughout the movie, leaders emerged, confidence was gained, distractions were removed, and their vision was cleared. Initially, the team's objective was simply to win football games. As time went on, they realized that the true objective was actually to strengthen their circle. Winning football games was simply a byproduct of achieving that goal.

Inspired by what I had seen, I immediately grabbed my journal and a pen and sat at the built-in desk of my dorm room. Within 15 minutes, I had written what I felt was the true representation of what your inner circle should encompass. Whether it pertains to your relationship, to your business, to your social circle or how you raise your children, it will always be the bond that reflects how your circle will thrive.

Bond of a Teammate (March 21, 2001)

You say that I'm dependent,
Sure, I like to lean.
When it's time to pick the captain,
I want you on my team.
I will not play above you,
Nor will I play below.
We'll play the game together,
And together we will go.
Places you could only dream of,
Places we have never been,
On journeys seldom traveled,
To be victors in the end.
I'll do my best to pick you up,
Whenever you are down,
And fight right there beside you,
Out on the battleground,
And when the battle's over,
You know with everything I tried,
It's true I may not need you,
But I want you by my side.

Bond of a Teammate
3/21/01

You say that I'm dependant,
Sure, I like to lean,
When it's time to pick the captain,
I want you on my team.
I will not play above you,
Nor will I play below.
We'll play the game together,
And together we will go.
Places you could only dream of,
Places we have never been.
On journeys seldom traveled,
To be victors in the end.
I'll do my best to pick you up,
Whenever you are down.
And fight right there beside you,
Out on the battleground
And when the battle's over,
You know with everything I tried,
It's true I may not need you,
But I want you by my side.

CHAPTER 10
LIVE BY THE "C"

Any structure must have a strong foundation. The cornerstones anchor the foundation. For some reason the cornerstones that I chose to begin with I never changed.
~ John Wooden

I've come to realize that many of the tools that have made me successful today have to do with living by the "C"—connections, consistency, confidence, communication, commitment, charity, and calendar. If you take nothing else from this book but apply these seven core principles, your life will be increasingly productive. These small changes to your everyday life will determine how you navigate through life.

Connections

Just as we discussed in our circles, our network, which surrounds us, is vital to our success. Many of our connections reside outside of our listed circles. Extending a multifaceted network means reaching across the internet and in person. This levels up the connections all around us like sonar waves. The internet is full of career advice sites, including indeed.com, that provide tips on how to develop and expand your connections.

"Networking waves" connect to your audience on a more personal level. These connections are typically in person and a little more intimate. They are people you see rather frequently. They are the familiar faces in your local Chamber of Commerce and at networking events like 1,000,000 Cups, church groups, country clubs, or even public speaking events. The engagements at this level will show more loyalty to endorse your product—you.

It's crucial in life and business to be front-facing and get your brand out there. Align yourself with the right people in order to grow personally and professionally. I'm not just talking about close friends and your inner circle, but all who will validate your product. The echo effect we receive from these connections is transmitted back with greater resonance. By "echo effect," I mean the closer the transmitted wave is to you, the stronger the echo is in return. An example is sharing your dream or story with someone in a local networking group, creating a more personal return and thus establishing a strong echo effect. As our waves reach out, we see a broader echo effect.

You're the keynote speaker for your product. Other spokespeople who advocate for your brand should be so compelling, so captivating, that all you have to do is step up and drive it home. Who is your proverbial entrepreneurial wingman? Right off the bat, you should be able to name a dozen. These individuals will speak highly on your behalf to help establish your credibility, so choose wisely. Like our team in the *Being Passive* chapter, more indirectly, we surround ourselves with other likeminded individuals who share our passion. We do this through networking.

Networking with the right people is the number one way to ignite your business. Put yourself in front of anyone who will listen. It only takes that one perfect fit to complete the puzzle and send your business soaring. Modes of networking include social media platforms that allow us global exposure as we share our stories with the world. The quickest way to hit the seven-figure mark is to surround yourself with those who will genuinely and rampantly spread your message and promote your products and services. Your brand will be much more enticing with third-party validation, recommendations, and testimonials.

Remember, I moved to Kansas City and knew no one, absolutely no one. I began building a brand and making connections. Once my connections were in place, I was able to make moves. I was in a transitional period in my life as a personal trainer, so I wasn't at a place to make huge advancements as far as opening a gym or hitting my seven figures. However, I was able to use my connections to acquire new clients, gain business deals with various companies and receive perks that would enrich my family's life.

I also utilize this technique to get a point across to my children. If I'm trying to get something through to my kids, I talk with a teacher or a coach to relay this message to my child. This works when our children don't want to hear what we have to say or feel they are smarter than their parents. There are also times when a parent prefers to "just be the parent" and not have to be the teacher or the coach. By creating this chain of third-party influencers, it no longer becomes lecturing or soliciting... it's validating.

Consistency

The strength of a brand hinges on consistency. If we are not consistently keeping track of our schedule, consistently avoiding dopamine responses, consistently problem-solving, and consistently filling our shopping cart with productive items, then we'll surely wander astray. Our ability to maintain a routine, day in and day out, determines our progress.

Let's say that you start a new routine that includes the goal of running a mile every day for one month. What's not so apparent within the first week becomes greatly apparent at the end of the month. Your ability to complete the mile has gotten substantially easier.

If, like me, you despise early mornings, what would happen if you forced yourself to wake up at 5 a.m. consistently for one month? You'd begin to alter your body's circadian rhythm, gradually making it easier to spring out of bed, rather than repeatedly slamming down the snooze button. Talk about consistency-forming habits! If we increase the number of productive habits in our lives, we begin to see immense growth and with it, the growth of our mindset.

We often find ourselves venturing away from the path of consistency when things begin to shift outside of the norm. If our routine is interrupted by negative or even positive distractions, we can detour from our intended goal. Sustainability over time is how we compound onto our success. Imagine you're making money hand over fist. The reality is that you still have to provide a great service or a great product to sustain this success. Otherwise, your position will be filled with someone who can. It's a formula with consistent ingredients— hard work and tangible results. Rinse and repeat.

During an interview between Kobe Bryant and Lewis Howes, Kobe discussed the importance of consistency in the evolution of his success. He mentioned creating a "menu" of objectives that he needed to improve on to compete at or beyond the level of his peers. On the menu were tasks like improving his mid-range jumpers, 3-point shots, and free throws. These all became easier through repetition. In the interview, he acknowledged the fact that as he reached 13-14 years old, when the other players were heavily reliant on their athleticism, he excelled through the fundamentals acquired through regimen consistency. This means we are consistently improving our craft. We are consistently outworking the competition. We are consistently striving to find our groove. It's not rocket science. Put in the work every day to be better than you were the day before. That's it.

Every progression toward our goal is a stepping stone which is fueled by consistency. When I was conditioning for any competitive sport that I participated in, I knew that no matter how bad I felt or how much it hurt, I just had to keep going. Someone out there was working as hard or harder than me, so I could not allow myself to stop. I remember many late nights on the track of my high school, well after everyone had left campus and the stadium lights were out. *Just pick 'em up and put 'em down.* I had to remain consistent in my workouts to continue getting better. As I progressed through the run, I would count the laps and convert them to a percentage. If I was running 5 miles, that would be 20 laps around the track. *OK, I have done 8 laps, so I am 40% done... now I'm at 15 laps, I'm 75% done.* I never allowed myself to stop. It was the consistency and the incremental goals that got me through the Hell that was conditioning.

Here's another way to look at maintaining consistency. Because I've made consistency a priority now, as a father, I am able to plant these seeds of success in my children. I noticed that my son Beckett wasn't showing the same interest in sports as other children, so I signed him up for drum lessons. In hopes of sharing something in common, I signed myself up for lessons as well and quickly realized the difficulty of keeping it "in the pocket." The hardest part of being a drummer isn't just moving multiple extremities at various speeds but maintaining the repetition of the exact same beat for the duration of a three-to-five-minute song. It's about being consistent. If the drummer is out of sync, then everyone is out of sync, which is why consistency is so paramount. We gain success by finding a winning formula and consistently repeating that formula without variance.

Initially, Beckett grew extremely frustrated with his inability to maintain consistency throughout the music. He avoided practicing at home, as it still appeared to him to be work. The tedious drills of metronomes and paradiddles required every bit of his concentration. It was not yet "fun". Night after night, I would require him to go sit behind his set and practice. Some nights consisted of a half hour of drilling and some nights consisted of free play in the form of White Stripes, Foo Fighters or The Rolling Stones. It became more apparent over time that his consistency and repetition had built confidence in his abilities. He became more excited to sit behind his drum set and bang away with precision and intensity. His consistency yielded greater confidence, which then manifested itself into pure enjoyment of his newly acquired craft.

Beckett preparing to go rock the socks off the audience.

Confidence

We've all heard the saying, "Confidence is key," but what I've come to learn is that it's particularly true in the life of an entrepreneur. Our confidence piggybacks off of our consistency. The more consistent we are with our preparation, the greater our confidence level will be. Whether it's training for an athletic competition, repetitively practicing a big speech in the mirror, preparing for an interview for a newly open management position after a ten-year tenure in the company, or rehearsing your lines in a major production, the more hard work you put in, the more confidence you will exude. Putting in the work to gain confidence in your abilities will undoubtedly move you up the ranks, but it's only half the battle. The presentation of your abilities is not only the display of your talents but rather how you carry yourself throughout the entire display of them. While sure, it may put you on stage, until you have confidence in your delivery, you will never stand in the spotlight. Regardless of what you set out to achieve, you must be fully confident in your abilities. These are the signs of a leader, a successful businessperson, and a truly confident entrepreneur.

"Ability" is defined by The American Heritage Dictionary as "the quality of being able to do something, especially the physical, mental, financial, or legal power to accomplish something." An example of being confident in your ability is an elite athlete making a clutch, game-winning performance. Referring again to Kobe, imagine him standing there, calm and collected on the free throw line, down by one in the championship. The voice inside his head telling him, you've been here a million times before. Trust your abilities. On the outside, he takes a deep breath, maintains his focal point on the goal, and remains fundamentally sound. How do you feel when you step out there prepared? What is your mindset when you know you've put in more work than the person in front of you? Why do we see these athletes like Kobe, Michael Jordan, Tom Brady, Muhammad Ali, or Derek Jeter constantly in the championships? It's because they put in the fucking work. They expect nothing less than winning, and then they do. In any facet of life, having confidence in our abilities is the ultimate game changer.

As the *Mindset* chapter explained, those who seemingly rest high upon the leaderboard all have a similar mentality, —a winner's mindset. Our mindset is the only thing that can keep us from reaching our fullest potential. If you're scared to lose, then you will never win.

Do not be bridled by "I can't" and "I'm not capable." Do not be held in financial and emotional restraints by the power of negativity, doubt or self-pity. Your mind creates that negativity, and it can just as well destroy it.

The difference between good, great, and elite people is their ability to obtain mental clarity and operate with true confidence.

A highly motivating technique that I've come to learn is imagery. I've always been confident in the outcome because I simply never see myself losing as an option. Never in my mind have I thought, But what if I lose? Every single scenario that could possibly enter my mind only prompted the same outcome; I was going to be successful. It's the intangible discussed in the beginning of this book and the only way of thinking for me. A winner's mentality is knowing you've won before you ever step into battle. It's as simple as, "Where do you see yourself in ten years?" Do you see yourself as successful? Are you imagining what it will be like to be handed the proverbial gold as you stand on the highest tier of the winner's podium? Your belief in your abilities, along with the presentation of those abilities, boldly supports your confidence in your results—your winning results...the standing ovation in our grand finale, only to be followed by encore...after encore. There is no "go big or go home" that gives you an out, an excuse, or an opportunity for failure.

There is only "go big" in a life of success. **There are no contingencies on success.** You just keep working. Didn't hit your goal today? Work harder! Didn't make the starting position? Work harder! Didn't get that promotion? Work harder! The confidence that you're going to go out in your field, kick this world in the teeth, and come out on top is what brings one to the forefront. This is where you expect and allow yourself nothing less than exactly what you're trying to achieve.

On the night of December 29, 2022, I was sitting in my living room with my buddy Adam, just kicking back, relaxing, and watching the end of the Alamo Bowl between Texas and Washington. My wife, Kathy, had just come home around 11 p.m. with our one-year-old, Maris, and our high schooler, Tyson. Kathy and the kids went into a different part of the house to allow "the guys" to have chill time.

Not even 15 minutes later, Kathy frantically walked back into the living room, looking panicked. "I'm pretty sure I just heard gunshots out front."

I gave her a dismissive look and responded, "It's almost New Year's Eve. I'm sure it's just kids setting off fireworks in the street."

Kathy proceeded to peek through the blinds of the front hallway, then darted back into the living room and said with an even more panicked expression, "Umm, there's a guy with a gun in our front yard."

I quickly jumped up off the couch, directed her back upstairs with the kids, and ran into my room to get my gun. I rushed out the front door like I was playing Call of Duty and stood behind a large pillar on my front porch with my gun drawn, Adam directly behind me. Across the street, in a neighbor's yard, was the silhouette of someone hunching over and standing back upright. Then "he" (I assumed it was a he) proceeded to do this two more times.

Squinting into the distance and trying to make out the dark figure, I yelled, "Are you okay?"

A man's voice responded back, "I've been shot!"

Just then, the figure stood up and rotated his body slightly and I caught the reflection of the emblem on his uniform.

I turned to Adam, "Oh shit, that's a cop! Take my gun."

I took off sprinting across the street towards the cop with complete disregard for any active shooter in the area. I apparently also had complete disregard for the fact that amid all the commotion, I managed to slip on a pair of slippers that had Santa riding a unicorn. If that doesn't exude confidence, I don't know what does. Adam ran back inside, put the gun up on a high shelf, and followed me out.

It was so dark that I couldn't tell where the officer had been wounded. I asked him twice, "Where are you shot?"

He only replied with the same thing he'd said before, "I've been shot!"

Adam and I put the officer's arms around our necks and moved him underneath the streetlight and the correlating street sign where he could call in his location. While he was calling, I examined the situation. Immediately, I saw blood bubbling from his thigh. All I could think was if that shot hit the femoral artery, we needed to do everything we could to control the bleeding.

I stood up from his body and told Adam that I was running back in to grab a belt from the house. Right then, Adam and I both noticed there was also blood coming from his right arm. Okay, two belts!

I made a mad dash back to the house, high stepping my way across the street, and eventually kicking off the slippers that were slowing me down. I ran into my closet, grabbed two belts and quickly returned to the scene.

I slid the belt beneath the officer's leg and wrenched it as tight as I could at the most proximal point of the thigh. I told Adam, "Keep pressure on that arm right at the shoulder while I cinch this tourniquet." As I was working to stop the bleeding, I heard sirens closing in from the distance. Just as I moved into position to tie off the arm, cop cars swarmed in from every direction like it was some kind of 80s action movie. Immediately following, the ambulance pulled up to the scene, and I backed away, allowing them to do their job.

I later found out the officer had been shot in the left thigh, missing his femoral artery by only a millimeter, and was shot in the right forearm, blowing out his elbow.

From the moment Kathy told us she saw a man with a gun to our rendering medical aid, there was no doubt and zero hesitation. I was confident in my abilities to control the situation based on the knowledge and training I learned in school and throughout my career. I understood the magnitude of the situation, but did not let that deter me from doing what needed to be done. And thus, The Slipper Savior was born.

Your confidence is yours and yours alone. You create it, strengthen it and control it. There is no one that can take it away from you because your confidence cannot hinge on the expectations of others. Confidence shall not be shaken by the insecurities of the weak. Feed it, nurture it and protect it at all costs. When you're prepared, everyone and everything around you is ambient. It doesn't exist. You are tuned in and focused on the goal.

Preparation + Laser Focus = Confidence

Communication

Communication comes in several different categories. Let's break them into five different categories—what to say, how to say it, when to say it, when not to say it, and nonverbal communication. These five aspects can be placed in three groups that I call *the message, the manner,* and *the mission.*

What to say and our nonverbal communication can be coupled into the message. This is what we are attempting to relay to the recipient.

Nonverbal communication can also be placed in the manner, coupled

Receiving the Courageous Citizen Award from the Mayor of Bryan, TX following the Slipper Savior incident.

Adam and me standing with Officer Watson and Mayor Gutierrez, accompanied by each of our families.

with how to say it. When to say it and when not to say it fall under our mission. I like to break it down into these categories to differentiate the aspects of communication.

Communication is the driving force that catalyzes our success rate by enhancing the way that we can present our ideas to the outside world.
First and foremost, you must know what to say. Everything else revolves around that. What is your message? If you could yell it from the rooftops for all to hear, what would you say? If you have a solid message, then your presentation of the manner and mission will naturally come to fruition.

To some degree, all communication comes with an agenda. The agenda can be as basic as being nice to a stranger to encourage happiness in their life. You can begin and end your conversation with a simple "hello," and to the right person, that can have all the power in the world. A simple "hello" to an emotionally broken stranger can have the power to add another day to their life, simply by letting them know that you acknowledge their existence and care enough to be attentive to their well-being. Knowing what to say can hold so much power! The right words, coupled with the right agenda, can take you anywhere you want to go.

Remember writing papers back in high school and college? They all followed the same format, introduction, body, and conclusion. Verbal communication is no different. Each component of the conversation holds its own significance. They are the building blocks necessary to formulate a message worthy of grabbing one's attention with specific intent.

The introduction breaks the ice, letting the recipient know who we are and to immediately gain their interest. This is your headline. What does it read? The attention span of today's individuals is minimal, to say the least. People want to be stimulated and they want to be stimulated from the very beginning. It's like that untrained dog on a walk. One second, they are trotting next to their owner, and the next thing you know, "Squirrel!" If you want your audience fully engaged, then you must remove all the squirrels that may run across your conversation as you begin an introduction. This is the time to facilitate the full engagement of the consumer or audience.

This is all forms of communication. Whether you're carrying on a verbal conversation or engaging through email, you must fully engulf the recipient. The average reader will read three words of an email or a text before they make the decision to continue reading on. What are you going to say in those three words that will encourage them to read on? Going through business classes, we practiced our "elevator speech." If you're in an elevator with someone for thirty seconds, this is where you pitch them your introduction. The question is, if you spit your introduction and hand them your business card, will they call you to hear the body of the conversation? This is the time when you capture your audience. If you're getting shut down in sales, you're not enticing the consumer in your introduction. They've already made up their mind before hearing the body.

This is where you set the tone. You stay on offense the entire time, even if you're listening. You set the pace of where you want the conversation to go. With that being said, they shouldn't want to talk during your introduction. They should be so captivated and eager for you to continue that they have nothing to say in those moments.

What did I do in my introduction to this book? It was quote after quote and meme after meme of material. My mission was to draw you, the reader, into the body of the book—the part that matters. But I had to get you excited about it first. What have I been doing throughout the entire book? Just as I did as a server, I'm kneeling next to your table and communicating on the same level. I intentionally write how I speak, seeking a conversation with you, seeking connection.

As mentioned earlier, all communication has an agenda. Believe me, my agenda is not to trick anyone into thinking I'm more intelligent than I truly am. My agenda is to relay information in a way that is helpful—something you can read and re-read back and forth through paragraphs and pages. My goal is to reference a multitude of creative and influential ideas to assist you on your journey. It's a dialogue, not a monologue. That is how I write, very conversationally, and I wish all self-help books did the same. There would definitely be more page-turning.

I had a coach when I played tournament baseball in my teens who visited the mound when I struggled to control my pitches and said, "You're just playing catch. Don't think about anything else, and play catch." You and I, as you follow me through this experience, are simply playing catch. Communication should be simple and relatable. There is no need for technical bullshit! Just be genuine!

Whether reading through a book or watching you at a podium, our audience should be on the edge of their seats. Here you'll have structured points that support your agenda. The objective is to flow through the key points of the conversation with very smooth transitions to effectively communicate your message. Your key points should flow from one into the next and subsequently build off each other. Invite your opposing conversationalist into the body of the conversation with open-ended questions.

This is a two-way street. Consumers want to be heard, too, so build rapport. I listen to my patients and lead them with their best interests at heart. They may have entrenched opinions that are detrimental to their well-being. I, as a chiropractor, have the ability and responsibility to offer multiple routes that will ultimately lead to the same medically preferred destination. This type of foresight will allow you to prepare your rebuttals beforehand as well, no matter your career path.

In many businesses, cunning salespeople (think bad wolves) play to their customer's attributes to engage them further. In other words, products and services don't always sell without some form of manipulation. For instance, if customers are driven by money, status, or even sex appeal, then the salesperson caters to this attribute and tells customers what they want to hear. These types of salespeople prey on impulse tendencies, which may or may not ultimately benefit the customers.

Is this on the up and up? In a perfect world, salespeople would identify what customers truly need so that they walk away satisfied. Buyer's remorse would no longer be a "thing," and the predatory label attached to salespeople wouldn't exist. Everything would be fair and square. It is possible to service customers honestly, keeping in mind their needs. Be honorable. Run an ethical practice. Put your customer first and the rest will follow.

Then comes the conclusion, where the deal is closed. Just as Alec Baldwin said in the 1992 movie *Glengarry Glen Ross*, "Always Be Closing"—the ABC of the sales. You've kept the listeners' attention this long. At this point, they are sold. They want and need what you're selling. Give them a place to sign on the dotted line. If you give them a decline option at this point, they'll doubt everything you've talked about throughout the introduction and body of the conversation. You're likely wasting your time. We just talked about confidence. This is where you exude confidence. You know they want to buy, you know they want to engage, so show them. Toss them a pen and let them sign on the X.

People often get caught up in their ideas and don't know how to relay it to the consumer. They aren't sure how to get their point across because they simply don't know *how* to say it. The accessibility to communication mediums is endless. I don't care if it's speaking, whispering, texting, emailing, sign language, or smoke signals; you must know how to get your point across. There are no excuses for lacking in communication skills. This is the manner in which you communicate your message, and it has to be crystal.

Relay your message in a medium that doesn't just suit you or is convenient but is the most effective for you. Use mediums that accommodate your skills. Don't hide behind texts, emails, and DMs because you're scared to deliver your message face to face. You're potentially overlooking a form of communication that could be very successful. Tap into it! If you can't relay the message, you can't be successful; I can't express that enough.

We talked about Becky in our *Your Perspective is Your Objective* chapter. This is a good example of poor communication. Remember how I said, "Her vast intelligence, in this case, is superseded by my ability to utilize mine." You can only be as successful as your ability to get your message across. This is an example of communicating logically, especially in difficult situations.

Difficult conversations can't be avoided. Many business decisions and conversations prove to be very difficult. This is when talking and listening skills really count. Always walk in your customer's shoes, especially when you're angry. Remind yourself how you want to be treated when you have beef. Apologize for any perceived problem, be receptive to the complaint, examine what part you (or your company) may have contributed to the problem, keep your voice steady, and see if it's possible to turn the situation around.

In my practice, I constantly interact with my patients. I am communicating verbally, reading their body language, analyzing functional movements, and diagnosing their condition. I cannot leave the patient in the dark on the "whys" and "hows" of their treatment. My mission statement says that I will educate my patients, so I make it a priority to honor that statement. It's the time I take to relate to my patient. I can take that time to be empathetic and understand my patient's needs so I can provide the most quality care. This, in return, creates retention.

When I communicate well with my patients, I often experience a directly related surge in my business. Cancellations drop to a minimal level and there is a good flow of the office. Although it doesn't take me any longer to explain to patients why I'm performing certain procedures, they don't feel as if I am trying to rush them out of the office. If I can accurately describe what they are feeling throughout the procedure, unprompted, without them disclosing the nature of their pain, then this not only provides comfort for the patient, but it provides credibility for myself. Everything is done for a reason. There is no wasted energy in our attempts to communicate with someone.

We've established the what and the how, but it's equally important to know when to say it. Knowing how to formulate a conversation dictates the pace of the conversation and determines where the conversation will go. You, as an entrepreneur, must know how to structure the conversation to keep the counterpart continuously engaging, all while leading customers toward the end goal.

A long time ago, I was in a communications class where the instructor gave an example of changing your wording to elicit the response that you want. She said, "Imagine a child running at a swimming pool and you were the lifeguard sitting in the stand. How would you get that child to stop?"

A male student responded, "I'd yell 'No running!'"

The instructor responded, "What do you think that child heard when you yelled that? They most likely heard the word 'running' and will continue to run, in turn causing you to repeat yourself more forcefully. What if you firmly said 'Walk, please'? We tell them to do something, or we tell them not to do something."

We present the same intention or direction, yet we elicit the desired response simply by changing our verbiage and tone. Another example I use is in preparation for adjusting a patient's neck in my office. Most often, patients tense up to guard their necks as a response to the vulnerability of someone handling their head. So, how do I get them to loosen up enough for me to do my job? If I am holding onto someone's head and asking them to relax, what do you think their initial reaction is? What would you do in that situation? It is my experience that nine times out of ten, they will do the complete opposite. What if I give them the precise instruction of, "Let your head fall into my hand?"

Just as we should know when to say it, we should also know when not to say it. You should not just be talking only to hear your own voice. What did I say? No wasted energy. Why are we muddling up our conversation with unnecessary dialog? Your message gets lost in translation and you're off on a tangent somewhere that is not just far from the point, but it's far from the sell.

We are going to talk about "running to daylight" soon. Every conversation is a pitch. Every pitch should find its way to daylight. Every line that comes out of your mouth and every gesture that your body elicits better have a purpose; otherwise, it's wasted energy.

This is a developed skill that very often is conditioned by your upbringing. If we observe the way a child interacts within a group setting, we'll typically see the inability to pick up on verbal and nonverbal cues that tell them when to enter or exit a conversation. Over time, with the help of numerous interactions, the ability to recognize these cues will be more apparent. Individuals with a considerably lower communication I.Q., or "I.Cue," tend to lean in one of two directions. On a more abrupt end of the field, they tend to blurt out, oftentimes annoying their fellow conversationalists and intruding on their time to speak.

One would think that this behavior would come from individuals raised in a larger family, fighting for their time to speak. I don't see this as accurate. The individual from the big family has had ample experience in recognizing cues on when to enter or exit a conversation. The only child, however, does not have this experience and will often be allowed to interrupt when the time is not appropriate.

At the other end, we have the individual who will often never be heard because they don't know when to jump in. It's like me trying to enter a round of Double Dutch. The two people controlling the jump ropes can be twirling them seamlessly, but I will still be stuttering on the side, not sure when to make the jump in. After all of the doubting and the hesitation, when I finally decide to jump in, I will undoubtedly bust my ass, because it wasn't the right time. The time for me to enter the "conversation" had come and gone and I missed it.

There are also people that exhibit traits from both aforementioned. The individual who is unsure when to chime into the conversation, causing them to be muted on the side, will still want to speak their part. Throughout the progression of the conversation, the individual will solely be focused on what they have to say, completely neglecting the ongoing dialog. At a point when they feel as if the conversation has come to a pause, they will interject with impertinent information pertaining to the conversation. This type of behavior will shatter any kind of credibility that you may have as a part of the conversation.

Twice a month I have a meeting with my therapist or a life coach, if you will. I feel that it is good to exercise the mind, not only the body. In my last session we discussed mindfulness and how it was lacking in many of my relationships, professional, personal, and otherwise. Oftentimes I find myself with patients who begin to describe an injury or an issue, and I begin to think they might be exaggerating. What I should be is empathetic because being empathetic allows me to relate. Leave the rest of the cards in the deck and play the hand you're dealt now.

You can run through a multitude of thoughts in your head, but only some things need to be spoken. Take some time to process what it is that people are saying and the best way to communicate your reaction to them. The key to strong communication and bringing further mindfulness to relationships is listening. Plain and simple. When you're in conversation, are you actually listening or are you just waiting for your turn to talk? Generally, we become distracted from effective communication because we are too busy formulating the next idea or rebuttal, when we should truly be listening to what the other person is saying. Get out of your damn head! Challenge yourself to listen in conversations and push people to engage in deeper conversations with you by asking open-ended questions. In sales, a simple yes or no answered question would be nice, but it doesn't always work out that way. What questions are you asking to get it to that point?

Lastly, you should always avoid fast talking if you ever feel that you're behind in a debate. This tends to make you look desperate and you'll typically speak wildly, losing the ace in the hole that you were purposely holding back. Once that ace is played, it's played. Most often it is played abruptly at the least opportune time, therefore diminishing your odds of the debate or making the sale.

Let's look at a hypothetical situation of two people in a courtroom. Both sides have provided their counsel with the most convincing information and put together what they feel gives them the best chances for their side to win the case. Both sides present all of their evidence, and the judge is persuaded in one direction to make a ruling. As the ruling is announced, the losing side quickly blurts out additional information in a desperate attempt to sway the final verdict.

At this point, the verdict is made. Court or sales, it is made. There is no fast-talking your way back to a win. The cards are played, and there's nothing else to do at that point. You can't throw an extra card down and hope the dealer doesn't see it. Simply exit gracefully and regroup. This scenario is also directly applicable to sales. In an instance that you do not close a sale, you do not fast talk. Go back, do your research, put together a better pitch, and present the deal again at a later time.

In Joe Navarro's book *What EveryBODY is Saying*, he states that 90 percent of all human communication is nonverbal. Nonverbal communication plays a vital part in our level of success. What we must ask ourselves, though, is what percentage of that 90 percent is our opposing conversationalist picking up? You picking up what I'm throwing down? Every person we engage with is different. There are no two people created equal. However, all people fall into subcategories that we can use to prepare our approach.

Do you remember talking about being approachable in the *Be Enticing* chapter? Taking a deeper look into what it means to be approachable is observing what nonverbal cues you're giving off to those around you. What responses are you getting? Simple nonverbal cues such as the listener leaning into your versus away from you can cue you in on their engagement in the conversation.

Let's take a glance at relating to our consumers and our colleagues by expressing similar traits that that group or individual possesses. What is enticing to them? The concept of mirror neurons exists in most primate species, including humans. These mirror neurons, which reside in the premotor cortex of the brain, are motor neurons that are essentially linked to mirroring your counterpart's behavior. Those who possess a greater number or possess the ability to access more of these particular neurons will exhibit an innate response to mimic specific traits.

Is there a connection between those who are successful and those who have the capability of unlocking more of the compartments containing these neurons and subsequently allowing those individuals to communicate on a different level than the rest of the population? These tiny communication powerhouses are partly responsible for monitoring the engagement of our audience, providing empathetic feedback, and relaying your energy on a level that is far deeper than verbal communication will allow.

Let's just say that you're walking down the sidewalk and you were to smile at a stranger. Their natural response would be to smile back. What happens if they don't smile back? Are they not happy people, or are they simply not wanting to engage with you?

I acknowledged this concept while having an unrelated conversation with a friend of mine. We were simply talking about geographical moves throughout our lives. As you know, I left Texas in 2000 to attend college in Missouri. Prior to heading back to Texas for the Christmas break in my freshman year, I left my parent's number with my roommate, who was originally from Missouri, in case he needed anything. This was before cell phones were as widely popular.

A few days into the break he called my parents' house, and I conveniently answered the phone. "Hello?" I answered.

"Is Jason there?"

"This is him," I replied.

He paused for a minute. After a moment of doubt and mild questioning to be assured that he was talking to the correct Jason, he said, "Dude, you don't even sound like you. You sound like a hillbilly."

Within three months of living in Missouri I had lost my Southern draw, only to bring it back upon my return home. Further into our stint as roommates he began to notice a trend. Spring came around, and I made frequent phone calls to talk Astros with my PaPaw.

If there was one person I could sit down and talk about the Stros, it was that man. He knew every player, every stat, followed their farm systems, everything. A few weeks into the baseball season, my roommate made a comment. He said, "I can always tell when you're talking to your grandfather on the phone, because you immediately talk with a huge twang."

It wasn't until this recent conversation that I realized those were my mirror neurons firing at rapid speed, allowing me to relate with him better. This was a subconscious bonding characteristic that I inherited specifically when talking to him. That is powerful!

Have you ever noticed that when a couple gets married or they have been together for a substantial amount of time, they begin to develop the same likes and similar habits and are able to relate to each other on a deeper level? The same applies to communicating on a professional level. If you cannot connect with the consumer, then you'll lose. Our ability to remove the disconnect between ourselves and the consumer directly reflects the level of communication that we are capable of producing.

These levels of communication are a derivative of empathy, placing two individuals or a group on a congruent wavelength. Will a motivational speaker appear stoic on stage, relaying a monotone message with absolutely no hand gestures? No! The speaker will use whatever dynamic gestures possible to captivate the audience. In that moment of captivation, the audience will feel one of two things. They will share the same feelings as the speaker, or they will desire to feel that way. With every satisfying exclamation, the audience will nod in approval and applaud their mirroring feelings. With every passing across the stage the audience will track intently, in an attempt to further relate to the speaker.

These nonverbal engagements are so effective in all facets of our lives. Again, referencing the *Be Enticing* chapter, do you remember me talking about kneeling down next to the table when I was taking orders as a server? This was me relating myself to them. I was putting myself on their level. I was not looking down at them and they were not looking up. We were looking eye to eye with each other and able to communicate on a more connected level. It was my motive to remove any sense of inferiority from the consumer to connect with them deeper. Subconsciously, their interactions mimicked those of my behavior, as they saw me as one of their own. These subtle, individualized changes in your mannerisms will allow you to orchestrate this choreographed display of behaviors between yourself and another. It is this innate circuitry that allows you to inherently connect with others.

However, it is conditioned "wiring" that allows us to reach the masses. This conditioning allows you the ability to speak with confidence, which we just spoke about, to access a sea of mirror neurons that will subsequently follow your lead.

Commitment

In the late 15th and early 16th century, exploration of the Western Hemisphere became more prevalent amongst European explorers. As legend has it, in 1519, Hernan Cortes, a Spanish conquistador, set West in pursuit of the colonization of what is now Mexico. Cortes and his men sailed upon several ships through the northern Caribbean Sea and landed ashore on the Yucatan Peninsula. When the fleet reached shore,

Cortes's army violently overtook the native coastal villages before embarking inland towards the center of the Aztec Empire. Upon his journey away from the glassy waters of the Caribbean, he turned to his men and gave them a stern order.

I can only imagine Cortes standing on the bow of the boat with his arms in the air in a very intimidating manner, giving the order: "Burn the ships!" Fearless of what lay ahead and now with no option to retreat, he marched through enemy territory as the ships blazed behind them. The Spanish army pressed onward, massacring numerous villages before reaching their destination in the Aztec Capital, Tenochtitlan. Cortes's attrition on the capital came with relentless ambushes of the capital and its surrounding allying cities and halting the line of supplies to their enemy. With the collapse of the Aztec capital, Spain claimed Tenochtitlan as its own, renaming it Mexico City.

This is the level of commitment that is needed to "conquer" each hurdle to reach your goal. When the time comes and the work is put in, there is no tiptoeing into the water. You must fully commit and jump in. The only way to get anywhere in life is by taking the jump and burning the fucking ships. Commit not just to our goals but the effort that it takes to reach our goals. That's what it takes.

We previously discussed our circles and the integrity of those circles. We've all heard the phrase, "A chain is only as strong as its weakest link." Your level of commitment to the group determines how strong of a link you are in the group. Are you willing to put in the work to strengthen the circle? Your commitment to the group should be an unwavering dedication in the pursuit of achieving the overall goal. On an individual level, that same dedication is congruent to the level of success you can ultimately achieve. Your commitment is not measured in monetary values. True commitment extends beyond short-term motivations. This is why we see many professional superstars peak early and fizzle out shortly after. They were committed to the money and fame rather than the craft. This has everything to do with intentions and motives. Be committed to yourself, your team, and your craft. Be the leader who people want to follow.

We have already discussed the outfielder committing to the ball in the *Be a Problem Solver* Chapter. Business is no different. Commit to that shit! Know what it is that you want and go for it. When regarding your personal relationships, same answer. Commit to communicating with your partner. Commit to the mindful scheduling of time together. You must commit to yourself, to your loved ones, to your team, to your patients and employees, never stopping at anything short of your exact goals. That, my friend, is commitment in a nutshell.

Charity

As an entrepreneur, you'll network and associate with people of all trades. Your ability to facilitate charitable acts, monetarily or otherwise, will become much more prevalent as you grow your network. And believe me, the fact that you're able to grow your network brings a strong sense of gratitude. It spurs you to give back. You want to bless others just as you've been blessed.

During my time in the Kansas City area, I religiously listened to shock rock DJ Johnny Dare from 98.9 The Rock's "The Johnny Dare Morning Show" every morning during my commute to work or school. The typical broadcast consisted of crude humor, entertaining interviews and wild shenanigans that would push the envelope of the always listening FCC.

As if being on the radio wasn't enough of a platform, Johnny Dare monopolized the regional rock and talk show listening demographic to create a platform that would allow him to sit high amongst his colleagues and reach an enormous audience. One would think that such a foul mouthed, motorcycle riding, long-haired individual would be a little rougher around the edges, but in fact, he was quite the opposite.

Johnny was one of the most compassionate and charitable people I've ever had the pleasure of meeting. On the air, he would often give glimpses into his childhood and how he really came from nothing, overcoming life's hardships and eventually becoming one of the most popular disc jockeys in the Midwest. Knowing what that side of life felt like, Johnny was not only compelled but was eager to give back to the community. He was grateful and wanted to pay forward his gratitude. His efforts to better the community spawned several charities, including his involvement with the Kansas City chapter of the March of Dimes Bikers for Babies ride and the Hand Up Campaign, which expanded on his Christmas charity, Hope for the Holidays.

This is the charity that really hit me. People wrote to the studio, expressing their hardships and leading into the upcoming holidays in hopes of what Johnny would say, "Not a handout, but a hand up."

Upon receiving the letters, he read them aloud on the air and contacted the individual to further discuss the caller's situation. "What happened? Do you have any kids? What are they wanting for Christmas? What outstanding bills do you have? What would it take to get you back on your feet?"

Once an amount was established, callers phoned in and donated to the cause. Some would generously donate a dollar amount, while others would donate their time and their trade. Mechanics fixed broken-down vehicles, plumbers fixed leaks, and local businesses donated food or useful items in attempts to smooth out a rough patch. Amazing! Johnny utilized his position to inspire people to help and better the community. A better community for one is a better community for all. What an amazing, uplifting, and life-changing endeavor for all.

Upon moving back to Texas and opening my own practice, I wanted to give back in the way Johnny gave back to the people of Kansas City. Okay, pretty much the same way. In November of that year, I announced through social media that I would be starting a charity event. After outlining the way it would operate, I had to come up with a name. I creatively came up with Hope for the Holidays. Don't judge me. "If it ain't broke, don't fix it!"

I opened my practice on September 6, 2016, approximately four months before Christmas. Consumed with startup capital and an operating capital that was barely being met in this infancy stage of business, I had nothing to personally give to the cause, at least monetarily. Still, I was grateful, and I wanted to give back to my community. Being a business owner and growing up in this city gave me a platform. I didn't have the luxury of being on the radio every day, but I knew how to reach a target audience through social media, and I knew how to use my resources.

When I announced the campaign, I asked people from Facebook to write in and nominate someone they knew who was in a tough place in life. Several entries filled my email inbox, and I was forced to narrow it to the three that touched me the most. For the next few days, I read each letter via Facebook Live and posted the actual letter for the audience to reference. I set up a GoFundMe page and instructed that all non-monetary donations be brought to the office to be accounted for, sorted, and wrapped.

The weekend before Christmas, the families were invited over to the office. I made sure to have the tree up and the office decorated to prompt the excitement of a Christmas morning with the family. In the back of my office, I set up tables and my staff and family cooked lunch for everyone. The added stress to my regular day-to-day schedule was worth every minute and every smile with those families. In the following years, people anticipate my charity posting in hopes that I'll do it again. Every year we have an outpouring of hospitality, from money donations to clothing, to bikes, to auto repairs, and eventually an actual car. You cannot put a price tag on the positive effect that this has on your business, not to mention your personal life.

When talking about financial goals, I've stated I want to make enough money so that I don't have to do anything I don't want to do. To add to that, another lofty dream is to make enough money to give it away.

During my first few years, as I mentioned, I had people write in to nominate families and individuals who needed and deserved community help. It got so big one year that I was almost unable to keep up. My office was packed with five families, plus my staff and family, adding up to nearly 40 people. I loved that I could change the holidays for so many. The gratification is immeasurable. Nonetheless, I felt we were spreading ourselves thin and not impacting the families as much as we potentially could.

During Christmas of 2018, I crossed paths with a family that really touched me. No matter what life was throwing at them, they kept smiles on their faces and went to any lengths to help anyone else in need. Some people just aren't dealt the cards that the fortunate are dealt, but they play it the best they can. I recognize that certain people were dealt all low, unsuited cards, but they make it work for them. I have had my rough patches, but I can always find my way back to a better life. Some of that is how I was conditioned to be and some of that is just the hand that I was given.

I have pissed many good hands away just for the excitement and know that another good hand will come around. But I knew this family might not get that chance without help. I wanted them, for once, to get to rake in the pile. We put all of the eggs into one basket for that year's Hope for The Holidays. There was no announcement of the event that year, no letters read online, and no narrowing down of the many families in need. I met this family through the office just a few months prior. At each visit, they showed their gratitude for my time and effort. Even though times were tough, they prioritized chiropractic treatment.

So, in early November, I decided to nominate this family as the sole recipient of the yearly charity. Throughout each visit in the office, I used my superb investigative skills to learn what each of the family members needed and wanted for Christmas. We discussed how things were going and Todd, the father of the house, confided that there would be little to no Christmas for the family that year. Their only vehicle had broken down, and they had fallen behind on a number of bills.

Rather than blatantly asking the amount of their rent, something I knew would make them feel ashamed or embarrassed, I instead called their apartment complex and inquired about rent prices. I calculated a month of rent, utilities, late fees, and grocery money. Then I wrote and posted a heartfelt letter nominating the family for my charity without them ever having a clue. Responses and donations began pouring in immediately.

As we moved into December, I revealed our plans to the family and requested they meet us at the office on the first Saturday of Christmas break. The lobby was completely packed with festively wrapped gifts. As my staff, my wife, and I proceeded to bring gifts over to the children, their faces lit up. This was a new experience! They eagerly opened their stacks of gifts, and then I rolled out new bikes for each of the younger kids and a refurbished computer for the teenage girl. The room was filled with pure excitement.

I then walked over to the tree to grab a final gift and handed Todd an envelope. His wide eyes quickly welled as he opened the envelope and beheld just over $1500 and a voucher from a mechanic to help fix their family vehicle.

"I don't know what to say. I did not expect any of this," he said. "You have no idea how much this helps our family."

The ability to change someone's life, even if it's through a rough patch, is something you cannot put a price tag on. The contributions to the family were enough to get them over the hump and into a good place. I continued to keep in contact with Todd and his family from that point on. We occasionally go to lunch, they attend my kids' sporting events, and even join us for a few get-togethers.

My oldest son, Jacob with Johnny Dare—Aug 3, 2014 in Kansas City at the Motley Crue and Alice Cooper concert.

Calendar

The world comes equipped with many moving parts and very few instructions. Imagine opening a box with a thousand pieces and no model or step-by-step guidelines to walk you through the assembly process. You simply have the tools that are required to do the job and that is all. This is exactly the way that life, particularly in the business world, will be. One of the most useful tools in the toolbelt is the utilization of organization. Having the ability to plan your day, your week, your month and even years to come will undoubtedly facilitate great success.

When planning, we are essentially creating an outline for our lives, just as I have outlined some of the chapters of this book that presented more difficulty for me to write. I would have words on a page with no flow and no direction. When I took a step back and restructured the chapter into an outline form, the content poured out of me. Outline your life. Life is a complex series of events that need structure. Success is a plotted course of strategically placed timely events. You cannot build an empire from vague, arbitrary goals. **Arbitrary goals create inconsistent outcomes.**

In the *Being Passive* chapter, we talked about utilizing your time throughout the day to generate the most productivity. If you're using one app on your phone, it better be your calendar—a brightly organized, color-coded calendar. It should look like a unicorn shit out a rainbow across your phone. Each color should represent a different category.

I currently have seven different colored categories occupying my calendar. It is a true rainbow! I have a shared calendar with my wife for our family's events; I have a shared calendar with my ex-wife to coordinate my sons' activities; a calendar synced to my work computer to maintain my work schedule; one that is linked to any Google or social media reminders, a color for work which includes me sitting down and writing what I have for you today; one for meetings; and finally, an untitled calendar for all of those "extras."

You should know exactly how your time is being spent throughout the day. It is so valuable to your success that you have things planned out appropriately, so schedule yourself for success. Eliminate the entries that drain you. For that to happen, prepping and "extra" entries should be placed strategically into your day. When I say extra things, this can be anything that may be unnecessary and set your day back. These are negative stimuli that keep us from becoming engaged in positive relationships.

We all have monotonous and draining daily tasks to complete, but they have to be done. This is what sets people apart. Do you have the drive to get up in the morning, get things going and do what you need to do? I've seen memes across social media saying, "Messy people are the most successful people." Bullshit! This meme was created by someone sitting in their mom's basement with piles of clothes scattered across the floor and soda cans crumpled up on every surface of the room. If you're going to be successful, you better be organized or find someone who will constantly organize your messy ass.

Messy doesn't just mean in a physical sense. If you don't have your schedule laid out for the next few days, then you're messy. If you aren't taking at least two minutes every morning to go over your schedule to prepare yourself for the day, then you're messy. If you're letting personal turmoil dictate how you're performing at work or operating your day-to-day routine, then you're messy.

Messy appears in many forms. You must learn how to clean it up or delegate to get it clean and keep it clean. I have a good friend, Laury, who owns Clutter Be Gone Designs, a business in College Station. She's made a career out of organizing messy people. I knew the basis of what Laury's company did, but I wanted a more in-depth company description to share with you. Here's what she said:

> *Clutter Be Gone Designs home and business organizing provides customized professional organizing services. We offer a hands-on approach to creating functional, stress-free and productive environments. We can meet any organizational challenge with innovative ways to help you get and stay organized.*
>
> *In our everyday lives, physical clutter represents mental clutter at home and even in our work environments. Many people take organizing as meaning that you have to get rid of or throw things away. This is not necessarily the case; most things can be kept if you are able to organize the location of where said items/paper/clothes etc. need to go. While there will certainly be items that you let go of or throw away in organizing, most of the items you want to keep means having a home, a place for those items to go, and developing a system that works best with your life and environment to stay on top of all of the physical clutter that can seem to pile up.*
>
> *While we are located in Texas, if you are in need of organizing help, please visit us at www.clutterbegonedesigns.com as we can offer phone consultations as well as web consultations.*

A few points stood out to me. First, the type of environment she wants to create is functional, stress-free, and productive. All three characteristics are attributes of a successful business and a blissful life. Secondly, she acknowledges the connection between physical clutter and mental clutter. Remember the guy sitting in the basement? He has no mental clarity for promoting success and simply creates a façade to excuse his laziness. Finally, Laury let us know how to find her. She was enticing and accessible. I can only assume that half of you paused your reading to look up link that she provided, and the rest of you jotted it down to reference later. Laury not only lives for but excels at working with people who want to be successful and provides the organizational toolbelts. Some just need that boost to get them going in the right direction, and she simply acts as that springboard.

CHAPTER 11
OBSTACLES

It is not the strongest species that survive, nor the most intelligent, but the most responsive to change.

~ Charles Darwin

I'll share one of the hardest lessons I had to learn when going into business for myself. It was the inescapable fact that numerous obstacles would present themselves throughout my career, whether financial, physical, emotional, professional, or personal. These obstacles were always going to be there, appearing in various forms and at various times. So, learning how to revel in the presence of adversity was definitely a learned trait.

We've all heard the saying "When it rains, it pours." In business, that's an understatement. Seeing the big picture and recognizing each crucial step in your overall plan will allow you to stay calm and focused during these particularly stressful times. This is when we keep our perspective intact.

An obstacle is only as difficult as our perception of its magnitude. How we perceive each obstacle presented to us in life is the degree at how we can overcome it.

At a young age, my son, Jacob, started playing baseball. As often as possible, we went out in the front yard or would head up to the park to throw the ball around and get in some batting practice. Jacob's stepdad frequently gaslit my son's efforts with comments like, "Oh, I never struck out when I played baseball. I was always the best on my team, and I never had to practice." This created a false illusion that led my son to believe his successes would come without challenges or preparation.

I had to have a sit down with my son and explain to him that this was not reality. I asked him if he had ever heard of Babe Ruth. He nodded his head. I asked him what he knew about The Babe. He said that he hit a home run almost every time that he would get up to bat. Thank you, Sandlot!

Jacob was proud that he knew this. Without trying to burst his bubble too much, I asked him, "Did you know that Babe Ruth struck out 1330 times? That is 616 more strikeouts than the total number of homeruns he hit." His shoulders slumped about a foot as I told him this. He asked, "Then how can he be the best?" I told him that even the best hitters strikeout, the strongest guys in the world can be defeated, and the smartest guys get problems wrong sometimes. Even the greatest businessmen have setbacks and failures. It took Albert Einstein over seven years to get the theory of special relativity down. This is arguably the smartest man in history that could not figure out a specific theory but kept attempting it over a large timeline until he got it right. Each strikeout was merely a minor setback, a learning experience. The Babe said, "Every strike brings me closer to the next home run."

Jacob's shoulders raised back up as he grasped what I was saying. I could see the encouragement in his eyes now that things were put back into a perspective he understood. This concept must be ingrained into a child's mind at an early age, or they will constantly feel overwhelmed with even the easiest of tasks. From a parent's perspective, it's okay to push your child to be the best, but at the same time, make sure it's their passion. Otherwise, they'll plateau with unreachable expectations and resentment. This is the start of living for someone else's objective, which we'll touch on in a moment.

Failure is a hard pill to swallow and can leave an undeniably bad taste in your mouth. Humility is an acquired taste, but both are necessary. Why? Because we can't fully appreciate the sweetness of victory unless we've experienced the bitterness of defeat. How do you respond in the face of adversity? Will it break you? Will you learn from it? Remember that difficult times pass, and the lessons forge better times in the future.

There's a picture I like to reference regarding the way we should approach obstacles in our lives. At the top, it says, "There are two kinds of people." The picture is of two glasses filled with water. On the left, a person is frantically reaching for the top, desperate to keep his head above water and all but consumed by what life is throwing his way. On the right, the same person is laid back, hands behind his head and peacefully floating atop the water. It's not that the person on the right has less obstacles to overcome. He simply understands that these obstacles will undoubtedly occur and is confident about overcoming them.

Someone who doesn't deal well with adversity will constantly feel as if their back is against the ropes. For instance, when questioned by a reporter if he felt concerned with Evander Holyfield's game plan, Mike Tyson responded, "Everyone has a plan until they're getting punched in the face." Granted, the fight did not turn out in Mike's favor, but we have to admire how Holyfield overcame the many obstacles preceding, during, and following the fight.

Yes, unforeseen obstacles will come at you. You'll think you have a solid business plan, then POW, life punches you square in the mouth. You might even get punches in bunches. How are you going to come back? One after another, you're either going to take it right on the chin, or you're going to find your way around it. When you feel like your back is pressing against the ropes and you're taking life's flurries head-on, the most important thing is to never allow yourself to be consumed by stress. If you can keep it together when things become increasingly overwhelming, then you'll see success.

You absolutely cannot get discouraged and let it throw you off your path to greatness. It doesn't matter how weak your legs may feel beneath you. Always remind yourself that you have the strength to move forward. This is where being a problem solver comes into play. Recognize the challenge in front of you and put together a game plan to get you through it. Life will continuously come at you, so find a way to win, every single time. Do not allow yourself to cower down and take those unnecessary shots. This will only leave you feeling defeated. The end game is the end game, period! If you know what you want, you have to "fight" to get it.

In the Storm

I was sitting in church one Sunday, and the pastor made a comment that really stuck out. He said, "When you're in the middle of a chapter of your life, you don't realize that it's a chapter. It's just life." These particular chapters in life feel like overwhelming storms in which you become engulfed. That is so true. There have been countless times when I'm in the middle of the storm and feel exceedingly defeated, but then I come out on the other side and think, *Okay, that wasn't so bad.*

It doesn't matter if it is a short-term thing like "Am I going to make overhead this month?" or "Will the stock market plummet today?" It might be something more personal, like going through a divorce (which can definitely affect how focused you are on your business) or losing a job. It might be something more long-term, like an illness or paying off student and business debt you accrued to put yourself in a better position. These are all valid concerns.

We have to put in the work and step-up toe to toe to make the best of any bullshit. What makes each individual different is how we handle those issues. In every story, there has to be a struggle for the protagonist to overcome. You're the protagonist—the hero—of your own story. Don't expect to be the exception. No one experiences smooth sailing throughout all their successes.

The following conversation is between a friend and me. I was about three months into practice and had already felt completely consumed with the stress of running the business. This was the first time I had had responsibilities of this magnitude. In my first business as a personal trainer, it was only me, a sole proprietor. There wasn't much overhead because I had not yet invested in opening a brick-and-mortar business, managing staff, or making payroll. I just had to go to work and cover my own expenses. That was it. When I opened the chiropractic office, I had those responsibilities and then some. It was a whole new world.

My family invested in my business to help make it happen, then invested some more to enable it to grow. I sat in a half-decorated empty office, advertising in every way I could imagine—TV, radio, social media, networking with other businesses, attending functions, and offering discounts. Amidst it all, I still had very few patients coming through the door. Random people mentioned that they saw me on TV, or friends told me that my name was the buzz in my field. Yet somehow, it wasn't converting to appointments, and I wasn't drawing the business I anticipated.

On a slow Monday morning, I struck up a conversation with my friend Michelle. As a fellow business owner, she had some good insight into the progression of the early stages of owning your own business.

Me: Good morning. How are you?

Michelle: I'm great! How are you?

Me: About as good as I can be, I suppose.

Michelle: Rut roh.

Me: Life is wearing on me.

Michelle: I have felt a little like that lately as well. Stressing?

Me: Yeah...business mostly. Juggling time for kids, workouts, networking.

Michelle: I remember those days. They were incredibly stressful. Juggling stinks. It's so odd to me how when we are in the thick of anything in our lives, it is so overwhelming. But looking back, it seems easier than what we are currently in. It always seems that now is the hardest. Does life just keep getting harder? I hope not. Maybe it keeps us on our toes because new challenges are always around us. New challenges seem super overwhelming, and once we've slayed the new challenge, it looks better from the other side.

Me: That's true, but then a new and usually harder one presents itself.

Michelle: So, we just stay in perpetual "overwhelmedness?" Huh...I think that's the way it is. So that tells me we need to rethink how we look at being overwhelmed. I am so guilty.

Me: I know...I just want to reach my goals. I know that I will create more, but I will have that sense of success.

Michelle: VERY GOOD!! Me too. It is just figuring out how to get there. I have accomplished so many of my New Year's resolutions this year in my work world and some in my personal world, too. It was after this that I started thinking about setting new goals for myself, both in my business and in my personal life.

Me: My thing is I always set the bar very high.

Michelle: That is a good thing! I do too. For me, it's quality in customer service and product.

Me: Building relationships!

Michelle: YES! That is part of customer service. Trust! Trust brings repeat business.

Me: True. That is something I am very good at and may be why my business is starting off slow. I am more concerned with building relationships and getting paid on the back end, rather than milking people's wallet for the fast cash.

Michelle: Yes...I found that too in the beginning. I'm not afraid anymore though. I give so much of my time and equipment for charities, I am good at what I do, or so I have been told, that I no longer have trouble asking for basics. Where I run into trouble is going over my set time frame, meaning I offer an hour photo shoot, do a two-hour shoot and then charge them for only one hour.

Me: That brings people back, but it can set expectations of getting freebies.

Michelle: It has... but has opened my business up. Two charities have brought me paying business following the events. I keep those things and shuck the ones I can no longer rationalize helping. My heart is too big.

Me: I know, I am doing this charity Christmas thing and hoping that it goes as well as planned. Anyhow, I have to go for now. Let's chat later.

Michelle: Hugs and smiles. YOU'VE GOT THIS!

You have the right heart. Keep perspective. Keep cruising.

Me: Thank you ma'am. Coffee soon?

Michelle: Yes!

A few things stood out in that conversation. First, you aren't the only one. You aren't alone on some uninhabited island. Although you may feel isolated as rain pours down on your leaky shelter, you have more resources than you're aware to help fix it. Knowing which resources to use for which improvement becomes crucial.

This conversation reassured me that a slow start can and will build into great success. When I was a personal trainer, some of my clients got utterly discouraged when only losing three pounds in a month. I reminded them that three pounds was an improvement. I told them, "The faster you lose weight, the easier it is to gain it back. A slow, progressive loss allows you to grow into your new body and adapt to the new lifestyle." As a new business owner, I had to apply the same principle. How often do we see athletes and celebrities achieve instant success and then file for bankruptcy within a short time? They had no obstacles that forced them to grow personally or professionally. They thought they had it made forever. Therefore, they didn't manage and "grow" their success and instead hemorrhaged money. If you're sitting idle, all the riches in the world will eventually dwindle.

Another point that she made was, "Trust brings repeat business." If someone trusts you as a person, then you can count on them for repeat business or referring someone to use your services. Trust is huge! I had a patient come in recently who said she had not been free of pain or been able to sleep through the night in years. I've known this woman since high school, so there was already a level of personal trust. However, she had never been to a chiropractor before, so the level of professional trust had not yet been established.

As she walked through my front door, I was standing in the front desk area. I noticed she walked very gingerly to compensate for her pain. As she made it into the reception area, she could not wait to sit down. She filled out her paperwork, and we went back to the treatment room. She sat nervously on the treatment table as we went through all of her history and initial exam procedures.

During the assessment, we went through a range of motion. I asked her to try to touch her toes; she made it just to the top of the knee. Just imagine a woman in this much pain on a daily basis, so much so that it prevents her from moving, playing with her kid, or even putting her shoes on herself.

Once a diagnosis was in place, we began treatment. She was tender to the touch. I could barely put my hand on certain parts of her back without every muscle in her body tensing up with the anticipation of more pain to ensue. I moved her into a side position and brought the "sweet thunder," as one of my old doctorate school clinicians used to say. Her eyes lit up as there was a loud, audible gasp. She laid there on her side until I helped her to a seated position.

I said, "Okay, let's stand up and repeat our range of motion. Can you please bend forward and try to touch your toes?" With ease, she bent down, and her fingertips grabbed onto her toes. She stood back up without any sort of antalgic motion (disruption in her ability to walk) and immediately put her hands over her face, sobbing.

I gave her a moment to let it sink in, then asked if she was all right. She dropped her hands from her face and ran at me with open arms. If you think I'm using the term "ran" as an exaggeration, you're wrong! Compared to how this woman walked in the front door at the beginning of the appointment, she looked like The Flash. She walked out of the office to her car, and I watched as she had such liveliness in her gait. Between the two of us, I don't know who was more satisfied. As I do with all of my new patients, I called her the following day, and our conversation went as follows:

Me: How are you feeling now? How'd you sleep?

Patient: I'm still feeling really good!! Woke up before my alarm, slept like a rock. Fell asleep easily and quickly and actually stayed asleep.

Me: That's good stuff.

Patient: Yeah it is. I can't remember the last time I was able to wake up, just hop out of bed and not sit there and wait until I got feeling back in my legs.

Me: Hopefully that continues. I will see you soon.

She had personal trust. Now, knowing the quality of the product, plus the follow up to show that I actually care about her wellbeing, she developed the all-important professional trust. You can't put a price tag on this. It would not matter if my prices increased 50%, if you develop trust with someone and produce desired results, then you'll continue to get return business.

The last point of my conversation with Michelle was about having the perseverance to overcome obstacles. She said, "You have the right heart. Keep perspective. Keep cruising." As an entrepreneur, you'll come across more obstacles than you can imagine. You cannot plan out every little step of the journey, yet you have to adapt to the obstacles better than the next person. Adaptability turns a good businessperson into a great entrepreneur. We'll talk more about navigating through obstacles in the next chapter, *Running To Daylight,* but recognizing that we have obstacles all around us is the first step.

Whereas the next chapter is in more reference to the running back in football, recognizing the obstacles is like the quarterback scanning the field before the play starts—reading the defense, making a quick decision, and calling an audible if need be. What makes a person successful is the ability to make the best of it. It's all about what you're made of. I love the analogy of the egg and the potato to represent how someone will respond to a particular scenario. If you drop an egg and a potato into a pot of boiling water, the egg will hard boil. The potato, on the other hand, will soften to be eaten in all its carb-loaded splendor.

While both objects respond appropriately to the presented stimulus, they present inverse responses. We talked earlier about the importance of being a problem solver. How will you respond to obstacles that continuously occur throughout your journey to greatness? The key is to recognize the obstacle quickly, calculate the risk efficiently and overcome it.

Obstacles that present themselves throughout your life may be right in your face. Other obstacles, inversely, may be buried within you. Many times, these internal obstacles will make or break your ability to succeed far more than anything external. Let's compare. External obstacles are those that society or our environment create. External obstacles are the physical clutter in your life and the chaotic messes that disrupt your flow. Internal obstacles are those that you create within you or exist due to past trauma. They, too, are clutter—old ideas, toxic relationships, and bad habits.

Overall, clutter is anything that doesn't support your better self. Flip Flippin describes this concept in his book, *The Flip Side,* as personal constraints. What are your constraining behaviors? How are they preventing you from reaching your goals? Do you have the courage to hit them head on? You must own up to them! People will use your constraining behaviors as weaknesses and attempt to tear you down. You must acknowledge the constraints to overcome them.

We must tackle problems with adaptability, and to do this, we must have positivity. Pessimism is the home of clouded judgment. Successful people focus on what makes them better, which, in turn, allows them to overcome obstacles more easily. They have a positive outlook and recognize opportune situations. They talk with others about their ideas, they complement the successes of others, they encourage others in their moments of failure, and they accept responsibility for their own faults.

Do you notice that all these attributes have the person moving forward in a positive direction? An unsuccessful person tends to be more critical and blames others for their own shortcomings. You are your only competition. You must keep your eyes on the prize. If one of your obstacles is a negative influence, then shut it out. This ambient noise should have no effect on your ability to "hear" the knock of your next opportunity.

Tune all the bullshit out! Imagine yourself sitting in a crowded restaurant with your best friend that you haven't seen for two years. Your conversation represents all of the positivity that inspires you to move forward. All the conversations going on around you represents negativity attempting to deter you from your goals. What you should be doing is listening to your friend and soaking in all the positivity from that conversation. If you find yourself listening to the conversations around you, you'll immediately find yourself more consumed with negativity.

If you're distracted, your friend (the positivity you needed), will realize you aren't focusing on him or anything he has to share. He'll clam up or leave, causing another negative experience inflicted by you, the rude friend. You cannot focus your energy on the negativity around you and neglect the goal sitting right in front of you. You're your own underdog (as well as your own hero), and the majority of people can sense your headspace. They know when they matter, and they know when they don't. With the exception of those few who truly believe in you, your tendency to alienate others is self-sabotaging. It's up to you to dig down and prove the doubters wrong.

Do you recall the time when my son Jacob and I had to huddle up under the blankets in front of the open oven to stay warm because my utilities were shut off? I did not let this get me down, but rather used it as motivation to never be in that situation again. We all go through bouts of highs and lows, peaks and valleys, but it's all about staying optimistic while you climb out of a tailspin. Keep your head up. When the head is up, it's focused on the high point of the mountain. Pessimism only stalls success. Negativity only builds stress.

Stress is another obstacle that causes internal struggles. People who are incapable of dealing with stress often implode from bad decisions, health problems, and unhealthy relationships. Abnormal amounts of stress lead to stagnancy and directly impact your ability to move forward. The key to the stress obstacle is removing the friction that prevents you from achieving your goals.

Remember the section of *The Dopamine Response* chapter that addressed inheriting positive stimuli to maintain productivity? Remove obstacles that prevent you from reaching your goal and replace them with positive stimuli. Positive acute stress is the combatant of chronic stress. Things like consistent workouts, healthy eating habits, positive relationships and recreational, active hobbies will better shield you from the negative, chronic stress that is often associated with entrepreneurship. This puts you back on the right track of becoming your most successful self. Find the antagonists in your life and destroy them. They are toxic to your success. If your antagonist is entrenched, then stifle it so it is unable to cloud your judgment or affect your work. If you allow others to dictate your choices, then you'll struggle to manage your own life.

I still use a quote I came up with many years ago pertaining to people or obstacles that stand in your way: **"The only control that you have is the control I allow you to have."** No one can make you be or feel a certain way, but you! Eleanor Roosevelt emphasizes this notion with her quote: "Remember no one can make you feel inferior without your consent." You control that! You can regulate yourself through the simple thought process of aligning with positive energy in all facets of your life. There is nothing that should slow your rate of success. You're the only one with a foot on the brake and the accelerator to your goals.

Imagine an obstacle course race that never ends. You're sore and you're tired, barely able to pick your feet up as you trudge through the mud. One after another, the obstacles keep coming and becoming more strenuous. You must keep pushing. The true entrepreneur understands even if you're barely moving, you must press onward.

Sigmund Freud once said, "One day, in retrospect, the years of struggle will strike you as the most beautiful." To me, this is looking back on the storm with admiration for your accomplishment and recognizing that the hard work made it even more worthwhile in the end. The goal is much more fulfilling when overcoming adversity.

Life molds us into who we are. We must enjoy and be appreciative of the time it takes to get to our end goal. Otherwise, it wasn't worth getting there in the first place and it's not your goal after all. Of course, you have to establish a goal or goals before you start your journey, or you'll aimlessly wander. It's always a good idea to step back and re-evaluate your end goals, as well as your current course on getting to them.

To evaluate your end goals, you have to understand the process it will take to reach them. We're in a never-ending chess game. There is no checkmate in life. The goal is to prevent the checkmate. There will always be obstacles that stand in your way, and setbacks are inevitable. There will always be outside glimpses of negativity, but it's on you and only you to set up your board for the best chance to win. It's a continual process that you put on repeat. If believed in strongly enough, it will pass down to tomorrow's successors.

The game will never end, so play hard.

CHAPTER 12
RUNNING TO DAYLIGHT

The only limits you have are the limits you believe.
~ Wayne Dyer

Have you ever had that moment when you thought to yourself, *What am I doing here?* It's not a good feeling. It's like wandering through life without purpose. Every move in life must have a purpose. In this chapter, I talk about running to daylight. Daylight equates to financial freedom, promotions, more time off from work, quality time with your family, or whatever it is that drives you to the next level. What level of efficiency will you utilize to get there?

I grew up playing several sports. My father pushed me to always be the leader, no matter the circumstances. In seventh grade, players were eligible to play tackle football. Without choice, my father's decision was for me to play quarterback. As far as he was concerned, it was the only option. "The quarterback is the leader on the team, and you have to be the leader," he said. It was so predetermined that he initially wanted to name me Aaron Allen because he thought it sounded like a great quarterback name.

What my father failed to realize is that due to both of my parents' sub-5'8" height and my stockier build, I would never actually excel as a quarterback beyond middle school. My athletic ability was the only thing that enabled me to compete. His decision for me to be the quarterback stemmed from "leadership" tunnel vision, neglecting to acknowledge my strengths and setbacks.

I can't call them weaknesses because my height was a benefit at specific positions and certainly in other sports. My father also failed to realize that actions, not positions, makes a leader.

My middle school was one of three that integrated into our high school. When we all arrived at football preseason camp for our freshman year, I realized that everyone else had hit their growth spurt, whereas I grew very slowly. Slow and steady wins the race, right? Disregarding this detail, I continued to pursue my position as the "leader" on the team… the quarterback. After about a week of camp, it was apparent I could not keep up with the new talent that had merged into the program. The head coach, whom I had known for many years, pulled me aside and didn't sugarcoat anything.

He told me, "Jason, you're moving to fullback. You'll get very little to no playing time as a quarterback, and you'll benefit the team a lot more in the fullback position."

I replied, "My dad said that I must play quarterback. I don't have an option."

He just said, "You can barely run the option, much less run the entire offense. Let me handle things with your dad." He saw the potential I had in a different position to make us a better team. My build, my aggressiveness, my desire to not be stopped, and my physical skill set were all more suitable for me to lead in a way I never experienced before, not to mention it was much more enjoyable to play to my strengths.

Gary Vaynerchuk states in his *Top Ten Rules For Success*, "Bet on your strengths and don't give a fuck about what you're not good at!" That is totally true and that's what the coach understood. Play to your strengths!

With that being said, which has nothing to do with the topic of this chapter, we have set the stage for a good lesson. I would say the most beneficial football advice my father ever offered was, "Run to daylight!" He told me, "Don't waste your energy pitter-pattering your feet to make your move. Make the move and go forward. Always run north and south."

Often you see great highlights of the gap closing on marquee running backs. They backtrack and run across the entire field to break free up the opposite sideline and score. They get to the endzone. They reached their goal, but less efficiently than how the play was designed, running North and South. They showed determination. Every play is set up in football (in any sport, really) to provide the most efficient course to score. The offensive guard pulls to kick out a defensive lineman and act as a lead blocker for the running back. The quarterback fakes a bootleg to cause the opposition to hesitate in their commitment to the football, or the running back takes a jab step in the opposite direction to let the play develop before pursuing the hole.

Whether you know what these terms mean or not, they all have one thing in common. They are designed to give the player with the ball the most efficient path to score. Life is not linear. There are many moving parts. You're not going to breeze into the endzone, just as you're not going to walk into an office and immediately be handed a seven-figure check. Life is dynamic and it's always moving, so you must move with it.

What an analogy for running to daylight. It's all about adaptability. Your average second-string junior varsity running back could line up behind an NFL offensive line and score with relative ease. **Preparation gets us on the field, and persistence gets us in the endzone.** Success never comes without resistance, and our persistence on the field makes us successful.

Said already, you'll face a multitude of adversity on the road less traveled. However, you'll find a lot more disappointment on "Easy Street." Adaptability to constant change allows you to overcome new obstacles. Passion breeds adaptability. If you're passionate about your goals, then there is nothing that can stand in your way. That, in a nutshell, is running to daylight.

I can hear my dad now saying, "The squeaky wheel gets the grease." He said this to me religiously regarding persistence. Make enough noise and you'll get some attention. Keep on knocking and you'll eventually get an answer.

I mentioned earlier that my dad told me not to pitter-patter my feet and try to fake out a defensive player. But if I did fake out the defensive player, Coach Waller, my old pee wee coach, would say, "Pick up your jock," meaning being caught with your jock strap around your ankles, unable to move. Coach Waller coached alongside my dad, by the way. That deer in the headlights, feet in the mud feeling, just before you get burned and give up a touchdown, is followed by hanging your head in shame.

Back to the pitter-patter. You're sitting in idle, waiting for a mistake to be made, and giving the opposition (life) the chance to tackle you, rather than moving towards your goal. How are we advancing? How are we being productive? We aren't! We're giving them a chance to set up and then knock us down. At the very least, they'll slow us down long enough for another player to tackle.

Why run as fast as you can on this giant hamster wheel called life and not get anywhere? Instead, you must explode towards your goals. Figure out how it is to get there and start moving. Slow feet don't eat! How quickly you get to where you want to be is determined by how fast you can pump those knees against the force of the opposition. How bad do you really want it?

Up Your Alpha

The entirety of this chapter revolves around efficiency. My freshman year of high school was the first year that my school offered a wrestling program. This was right up my alley. Although I was a freshman, no one else had ever wrestled on my team, so it was a level playing field. We were all learning the same techniques for the first time. As an inexperienced wrestler, you tend to grab onto your opponent's head and arm, fight to position your body for maximum leverage, and try to throw him across the mat. The loud thud of him slamming into the mat is exhilarating. The problem is that it exerted a lot of energy to get into the position for the throw, not to mention using your opponent's momentum against him to execute that beautiful throw. Also, for the inexperienced wrestler, the probability of completing the move is relatively low, not to mention you're left in a vulnerable position when you fail to execute the move properly. There are a lot of variables that must align for the throw to happen.

Between my sophomore and junior year of high school, I attended a week-long wrestling camp at Oklahoma State University. It was life changing. I learned the importance of setting up and shooting on my opponent. At first, my inexperience left me looking very uncoordinated and ultimately defeated. I could not get it; it just wasn't clicking in my head. I was trying to initiate my shot from feet away, giving my opponent ample time to recognize what was coming and the capability to defend it.

One of the OSU wrestlers, who was assisting with the camp, noticed that I was struggling and stopped by to correct my mistakes. He didn't say, "Hey, you're doing this wrong." He said, "Hey, let me show you a couple of things to make your shot more efficient."

Efficiency! That's what I needed. He had me get in my stance and got in his stance in front of me. For one, he was not feet away. He was practically forehead to forehead with me. He asked, "What will you do if I do this?" and he shuffled his stance to the right.

I rotated to my left by moving my right foot forward to keep him in front of me.

He said, "I made you do that." He had my interest, but I was still not sure what it all meant. He said, "Let's do it again, but you react to my movement, rather than me telling you to move." He shuffled to the right, and I rotated to the left...oh wait, no, I didn't. As my lead foot, which is my right foot because I'm a southpaw, was suspended in the air for a fraction of a second to make my rotation, he timed it, dropped down, and pulled my leg out from under me.

Without any other setups, he used my natural reactions against me to complete his move with minimal effort. From that point on, the game changed for me. He proceeded by showing me how to use wrist control and movement of my opponent's head and arms to assist with forcing them to do what I want them to do. It was a fucking dance! I just had to lead the dance.

Basically, what I learned to do was "up my alpha." No, not in a socially aggressive way. Not even in a hyper-masculine way. Rather in an assertive, strategic way that allowed me to effectively dominate my field! In my case, "upping my alpha" meant building on my talent regardless of the objective, whether it was sports, business, life or whatever. It's about your mentality. I just needed to know how to unleash and harness it. It took training and mentorship.

You see, in my freshman year of high school, my coach nicknamed me Pinto because he said I had the gas tank of a Pinto. Win or lose, I was left completely exhausted in the middle of the mat. It was because I was exerting all my energy, succeed or fail, to complete one move. Whether or not I ended up in the dominant position, all my energy was depleted.

There were matches early on in my career where I would just lay there, completely exhausted, and just fight not to get pinned. There was no offense or forward progression, solely defense. As I learned to shoot, I was able to achieve the dominant position with plenty of "gas left in the tank," so to speak. Of course, the name stuck throughout my career until I changed my ways.

Everything changed dramatically after wrestling camp, and I became an updated model of my former self. From that moment on, I had the approach of "Offense is the best defense." I didn't let up, and I didn't give my opponent a chance to relax or recover. I was in your face at all times. I found myself flowing through tournaments a lot more competently and effortlessly. I was setting them up and taking them down. I learned to build on what I had already accomplished and take it to another level.

As I got older, I transitioned from wrestling to jiu-jitsu. Being a collegiate wrestler, I had a distinct advantage over other competitors at my experience level, but I noticed a trend in the higher-level competitors. They knew how to relax. I would go and go and go, and they would just ride out the storm. Time, once again, to "up my alpha", only this time it took on a new meaning.

I find it fascinating to talk with others regarding their approach to life and interpreting their thought processes. I was having a conversation over dinner with one of my jiu jitsu teammates, Mark Ryan, and his theory of running to daylight was a little more passive than mine, but it worked for him. It was very insightful to hear his approach to the game. Training together regularly, we know each other's tendencies on the mat. He knows that I will establish control early and continue to grind.

Mark then said something that has resonated with me to this day. He said, regarding our energy expenditure, "I don't have to be rich. I just have to get you to spend more money than me."

Wow! We talked about it earlier in *Your Perspective is Your Objective*. He distributed his energy efficiently to give himself a better opportunity to win.

Energy Efficiency = Success

I still use my "Offense is the best defense" mentality but incorporate Mark's "energy" efficiency process as well. I took the time to practice these newly acquired techniques, and they allowed me to become a more well-rounded athlete (and a person). Pinto 3.0, engage!

These are all sports examples that can easily pertain to the professional world. An experienced businessperson will know when to apply force to execute the plan and when to exude patience to allow for the plan to develop. Opportunities will come, and seeing them is much easier when you're not running full throttle.

I like to call this "sacrificing the pawn." Every endeavor you pursue will begin with a strategically thought-out plan. I am not the most proficient chess player, but when I do play, I use a very sparing strategy. I will sacrifice my pawns to put myself in a more superior position to conquer my goals. My pawns are expendable. Think ahead a few moves, get your ducks in a row, and utilize the plan. This applies to business as well. I am not saying that people are expendable. What I am saying is that if they are placed in the proper positions, this allows us to proceed to a more superior position. All people have worth, and you can learn something from anyone.

Let's put this into a real-life scenario, shall we? You're the ball carrier. You've recently opened your own business. You've built out your office, you've decorated, hired your staff, and you've got a business plan in place. You have now put your plan into action, and people are walking through your door. Before you know it, you have a steady flow of business and life seems to be cruising along.

Is that going to carry you through the next 50 years? Are you setting up your business to adapt to the next push of new technology to avoid becoming obsolete? Being constantly aware of consumer services and trends is another way to "up your alpha" in a business climate. Again, it's about learning and building on your strengths. What are all the trajectories your business could take in the brave new world of online opportunities? I was in a conversation recently about how retail businesses are dropping by the wayside due to online shopping sites like Amazon and Etsy.

An acquaintance said, "Ten years ago, I never would have imagined the internet monopolizing the way people make their purchases. Even grocery shopping online has become a way of life."

I replied, "I need to figure out how to get chiropractic sold through Amazon." You think it's silly now but mark my words; it will happen if it hasn't already. Maybe not in the physical sense, but more so than just general advertising, websites, and social media branding. The future will become so tech-heavy that most brick-and-mortar businesses will become obsolete.

My family currently uses a general practitioner who solely schedules online and does telehealth appointments or house calls if the situation calls for it. I could do this as a chiropractor, but carrying my portable table around is not something I enjoy. Been there, done that. He completely cut out the check-in and check-out process of a doctor's visit. He minimized staff, minimized overhead, and eliminated the need for the endless babble that comes with scheduling an appointment. He utilized technology to maximize his business with minimal effort.

People want convenience. My father is a home builder in the same city I live and practice in. When it comes to technology, he's a caveman. Aside from searching through videos on YouTube, he is extremely limited, and I'm talking prehistoric. To add photos of his homes to his website, he has someone take pictures, has a web designer upload them, and spends whatever time and money to add ten new images on his site.

I suggested he open an Instagram account, put a link on his website, and just take pictures daily himself. This takes little to no money, minimal effort, and he can control what's on his page. I even offered to write his hashtags, then explained it's the symbol also known as the pound sign used as an organizer for search topics throughout social media. With the right combination of hashtags, you can tic-tac-toe your ass right to the bank. The efficiency and practicality should be a no-brainer, but some can't seem to adapt and, therefore, fall behind. My dad's business, from what I see, is doing well, but has reached nowhere near the potential that it could with a strong social media backing.

Touch it Once

Many times, we tend to overlook the little things that become the most crucial, much like the numerous concepts in this book. It's the little things repeated over and over again that make a huge difference in the global outcomes of our successes. Much like our previously noted, incremental steps towards achievement, these disciplinary daily habits allow us to navigate through life more seamlessly. Our ability to maintain discipline with these tasks creates the foundation of our daily schedule. Abraham Lincoln stated that "Discipline is choosing between what you want now and what you want most." Strategically implementing these productive habits throughout your routine will yield productive outcomes.

When we set new goals, the appropriate habits must be put in place to create a framework that makes that goal achievable. Want to make more money? Implement strategies similar to those discussed in *Brick by Brick*. Want to get stronger or get that six pack back? Start a new workout routine and begin meal prepping. No matter what your goals are—getting healthy, getting sexy, getting rich—those are all byproducts of discipline.

In *Make Your Bed: Little Things That Can Change Your Life...And Maybe the World* by Admiral William H. McRaven, he outlines practical life lessons drawn from his experiences as a Navy SEAL. The central theme revolves around the idea that small, disciplined actions, such as making your bed every morning, can lead to greater success and resilience. McRaven distills his insights into simple principles, illustrating how they can contribute to personal growth and the ability to overcome challenges. The book encourages readers to adopt a mindset of discipline, perseverance, and attention to detail in order to achieve meaningful goals.

Performing these tasks routinely until the point they become automated will give you a sense of pride, which encourages you to move forward with implementing new, productive habits.

Upon getting married, my wife and I blended our families to create a modern Brady Bunch. If you recall, our household currently consists of me, my wife, and eight children (I had four sons, she had two sons and a daughter, and we welcomed our first mutual child, our daughter Maris, four years into our relationship). These eight wild, rowdy, fun-loving kids oftentimes fail to clean up after themselves, turn off lights, straighten their rooms, etc. Anyone with multiple kids can attest to the fact that they like to make messes, and not just any messes, but cyclones of disaster. I'm the kind of person with anxiety through the roof if something is not cleaned or is out of place. I crave organization and structure. Deep down, children want this same type of structure in their lives, regardless of how defiant they are to it.

To promote more of this atmosphere, I implemented the "touch it once" rule. For example, if you get a box of cereal out of the pantry, do not set it on the counter after pouring your bowl. Most of the time, you'll forget about it or just lazily leave it there. Have your bowl ready, get the cereal out of the pantry, fill your bowl, close it up, and put it right back in its place.

As simple as that sounds, my kids still leave the cereal box on the counter. Why do we waste steps in setting the box down? Why do we procrastinate and say we'll do it later? And for the kiddos, why do they want me to get onto their butts? The shortest distance from point A to point B is a straight line, so why add a point C?

As we progress further into our marriage, and more importantly, the hectic nature of our careers, it is absolutely essential that we maintain order in the household. Our children wake up in the morning, grab their laminated checklists from their holder, follow the order of tasks listed on the sheet, and mark them off one by one before breakfast. Upon finishing their breakfast, they complete the list and place it in the holder near their backpacks before leaving the house. The same routine is performed in reverse just before bed, with the list being placed back in its original holder.

These tasks, as we make our transition from child to teen, from teen to adult, and then again from adult to successful entrepreneur, will continually change over the course of time. As you get older, more and more is added to your routine. The tasks themselves will become more demanding and the consequences for failing to accomplish them becomes increasingly more severe. However, the earlier we choose to implement these necessary tasks to streamline our success, the sooner we will condition ourselves to travel down more productive paths.

Our efficiency comes from stringing together these tasks until our day is filled with productive habits. We've already discussed consistency and the importance of our calendar. How does our discipline differ from those two things? Our tasks may not always be tangible items that can be checked off upon completion. Much of our discipline comes from our attitude, our focus, and a deliberate objective to be joyful. *Atomic Habits* by James Clear states that the compounding of these habits will result in productivity, knowledge, and relationships. Setting up a positive structure helps rid your life of those egregious dopamine time wasters.

Clear also discusses the habit loop and how it will create results. The loop consists of four components; the cue, the craving, the response, and the reward. These are broken into two categories: the problem phase and the solution phase. In the problem phase, we begin any habit with a cue, which creates awareness of a situation and triggers the brain to act accordingly. The craving will then begin to make that action more "attractive." As we enter the solution phase of the loop, we have our response. The response is where we actually perform the habit, overtime making the task easier. The reward phase concludes the loop, which makes the task more satisfying. This operant conditioning, much like Skinner's experiments of behavioral motivation, will continue on a feedback loop until the habit becomes second nature.

It's all about being efficient in our actions and disciplined in our routine. It requires less energy to complete the task when you consider that you must eventually finish it later anyway. Just as it tends to occur in business, this pitter patter becomes a series of unnecessary steps in reaching goals—a senseless deterrent. It has taken a while for my children to pick up these habits, but learned behaviors, if consistently reminded initially and shown by example, will carry over into their adult lives and promote success and efficiency.

CHAPTER 13
THE FIRST AND SECOND MOUSE

---

*The only real mistake is the one from which we learn
nothing.*

~ Henry Ford

In life and business, we all undoubtedly make an abundance of mistakes along the way. As we travel throughout our journey, we'll be introduced to a multitude of entrepreneurial riddles that often require some trial and error before we finally get it right. Remember my conversation with Michelle? You have to remember that you're not alone in your struggles.

It is crucial in our endeavors that we recognize our mistakes and the mistakes of others as opportunities to grow. The successful entrepreneur understands that you can learn from anyone and anything at any time. The answers are out there if you open your eyes to truly see them. Life is one continuous loop of modeled behavior. The model is the "first mouse" in our lives. We consciously and subconsciously find ourselves in the position of the "second mouse."

I love the story of two mice who sit in the doorway of their little mouse home while eyeing a piece of cheese across the room. Each mouse represents two different entrepreneurial types and their approach to reaching their goals. The first mouse has his eye on the prize, that ever-tempting piece of cheese just sitting there for the taking. The problem? He let the prize distract him. He should have considered and addressed potential setbacks in order to be successful in his tasty endeavor. As he approached the cheese, salivating with eager intent, the trap slammed down and crushed his hopes and dreams, literally. It's the mistake he can't bounce back from.

Observing the failure of the first mouse, the second mouse cautiously approaches the trap, tests its functionality, understands the first mouse's mistake, and triumphantly acquires the prize. See what difference it makes when you simply break down the problem before jumping in head first? Viewing the overall situation from each person's standpoint and recreating the scenarios to fit your lifestyle and vision can make all the difference in success versus failure. The analogy applies to life in general and your business model specifically.

Oftentimes in business we see the successes of entrepreneurs who play the part of the second mouse. Did they overlook the "lessons" evident in the many failures of the first mouse? No, they absorbed and applied the lessons. Now, let's dig a little deeper into the scenario of the two mice. If we analyze each of their qualities, we'll see that the first mouse is ambitious in the pursuit of his goals. He's up and eager to execute. But he's unprepared and unaware of the potential setbacks that await in the shadows. He's overlooked the hangups. He lacked a well-thought-out plan. With no blueprint in front of him, he commits the most errors. He failed to lay the foundation of an idea and work to build it up and make it real.

The second mouse is also very ambitious but makes a point to be observant of the mistakes committed by the first mouse. He learned from the errors of his doomed predecessor and capitalized on the results. He has gained both knowledge and an example of what *not* to do.

From the time we enter this world, we are conditioned to think, act, and respond in a certain way. Positively or negatively, we are constantly being molded. It is up to you to determine which behaviors you'll mimic and which are nonproductive. Use the position of the second mouse to your advantage.

A lot of entrepreneurs, and people in general for that matter, tend to overlook the blessing it is to be in the second mouse position. Then they stall out. The second mouse is given a map that leads from your starting point to your goals, listing the mistakes committed by those before you, offering alternate routes, and engaging in opportunities. This is succession. We are all successors in our own right. We have to be able to recognize, acknowledge, and accept it. But we cannot assume there won't be potholes along the way.

In my last trimester of doctorate school, I was eligible to take a preceptorship, a position of practical training. Knowing I was going to move back to my hometown, I set up a few interviews with local offices to begin making a name for myself in the community. I walked into an office in the middle of a transition to a newer location. The main doctor was out on vacation, but I shadowed her associates for a few days, leaving a good enough impression for them to give a favorable report back to her when she returned.

Sitting in my apartment in Kansas City, I received an email stating they had accepted me for the preceptorship position. I was ready to get back home and get to work. Now, let's rewind a year or so. One of my mentors, Dr. Michelle Robin of Your Wellness Connection, ran a super successful practice in Shawnee, Kansas. I sought her out at the beginning of my doctorate career to begin getting some business insight. I contacted her and requested a meeting over coffee. Without hesitation, she was happy to sit down with me. She was genuine, she was unintimidated, and she saw something in me.

I asked if it would be okay if I came in to shadow her for a few days. Someone with that level of success was someone I wanted to learn from. She was an amazing person, was a great entrepreneur and kept her business close to her heart. Literally! She not only hugged every patient who came, but had them hug with their heads on the right side so they were heart-to-heart. Wow! I was taken aback by how much her patients loved and respected her.

I shadowed for a few days before I applied for a chiropractic assistant position at her office. I filled out the typical application and was then handed a personality profile to fill out. She called me the next day to come in for a meeting. We sat down, and I remember plain as day what she said.

"Jason, you're going to be a great doctor one day, but your personality profile rates you as highly dominant which conflicts with the flow in this office. This is my dream, and I have to be careful who I let in."

I didn't get the job, but I learned a valuable lesson about choosing a team according to your vision and your principles. An unsuccessful person would have taken nothing from that situation, other than "I didn't get the job." There's always a silver lining. I found a win in my loss and grew from there. I, too, would someday be selective in my future role as a chiropractor, hiring my own team.

I got back to Texas and finally sat down with the main doctor of the office who had offered me the preceptorship. We met for lunch, along with one of her associates. She tossed an associateship contract toward me on the table, having no idea who I was. She was a lot more impulsive and took a completely different approach than Dr. Robin.

After I agreed to a position as an associate with the office, I went back to my school before graduation and had to do an exit interview with the clinic director. He asked me what my plans were after graduation. I revealed that I had accepted an associate position. He looked puzzled. He asked, "Really? You don't want to open your own practice?"

I replied to his surprised inquiry, "I'll own my own practice one day. At this point, I haven't learned what I need to make a successful practice."

Going through school, we were given only one business class. There is no way to learn the ins and outs of running your own business in just a few months, not to mention insurance, billing, etiquette, and marketing. I was with the practice, including my preceptorship, for seven months—not a very long time in the grand scheme of things, but enough time to pick up on a number of things I *should not* do in practice.

The doctor I was associating with had been in practice for close to 30 years and it showed. She had built a solid patient base, but business was totally stagnant. To give you an overview of the operation, the front desk area was run by three to four people, not including the doctors—one person to check in, one person to check out, and two "flow" people.

The practice could have easily been run by two people if done efficiently. Patients walked in and picked up a clipboard to handwrite their daily intake. This intake form was taken by one of the workers in the front and placed on a back counter until they were ready to take the patient to an open treatment room. Once the patient was taken to a treatment room, the "flow" employee took vitals and/or began the client's scheduled treatment.

The chart was placed rear-facing in a tray on the door. The treating doctor was notified when the patient was ready. The doctor then handwrote any notes pertaining to the patient's visit, treated the patient, and walked them up to the check-out desk. The doctor was also required to circle the correlating codes on the back of the sheet, but that was remembered maybe half of the time.

Since these codes were required for checkout, a front desk person had to track down the doctor to close the patient out. Once the patient was checked out, the intake paper was put in a tray for the front desk to do a final review. When the sheet was complete, the paper was scanned and uploaded to the "flow" computer. The owner of the practice did not want to spend money on an electronic health records system, so she opted to use a free (and very confusing) scheduling system, a ledger, and a Dropbox to store patient files.

How many steps were taken to complete this process? How many chances for error? Her thought process was so focused on "Keep the computer programs as cheap as possible" that she completely overlooked the fact she was spending more in wages for extra employees, cluttering the front desk area, and wasting time instead of seeing patients because of the length of the process.

Taking a mental note of all of the unnecessary steps, I made an early decision to go as paperless as possible. We have the technology to do anything we want in this world, so why not use it? Before getting overly busy, I had one front desk employee and occasionally an intern to act as a "flow." My patients came in and filled out their intake paperwork via a survey on a tablet. The program I paid for monthly was customizable and allowed the patient's answers to be populated directly into their notes. Not only did this cut down on the amount of clutter sitting at our front desk, but it cut down on the time I had to sit in the treatment room and verbally ask the same questions, which took three times as long to get the same answers.

This allowed me to minimize the number of employees I had to pay and maximize the number of patients I could see in a day. After three months of preceptorship and four months of employment, it was apparent my fit with this practice was not good. It took them approximately seven months to realize what Dr. Robin realized in about seven minutes. She saw I was meant to be a leader, not a follower.

I didn't conform to the new office's policies, and I could not grasp their order of operations. To them, it worked just fine, but to me, it seemed irrational. Ultimately, I was let go from the associate position and was unemployed. I always wanted to run my own business, but I also knew that after graduation, I wasn't in a financial position to get things off the ground and running.

Like Dr. Robin excusing me from "her dream," I saw a silver lining in this opportunity. This was the fire that needed to be lit under my ass. It pushed me to be a business owner, so I took it, and I ran with it. I immediately put rubber to the road and began developing what would now be a successful practice. I was nervous, but I did not let that deter me from pursuing my own dreams. I had been a business owner before, but never with a storefront, major equipment, business loans, employees, the whole works.

I knew it was necessary to compose a solid business plan to plot my success, but also ensure steady growth as a business owner. I took what I learned from my mentors to put together the roadmap that would support my vision, not just of the practice, but where I wanted to go in life. I also knew that in order to grow beyond the practice, I had to acquire additional first mouse mentors who would help pave the way for my success.

In the spring of 2023, my wife and I were toggling between a number of investment ideas. In the midst of considering a slew of deals, we were approached by a current business/franchise owner to take over their less than two-year-old, already successful business. Christi Voelkel and her husband Tyson were the owners of a HOTWORX franchise in Bryan, Texas. One day I received a text message from a number I did not recognize. It was Christi. The text introduced herself, thanked me for being a member of their gym and asked me if my chiropractic office would like to set up a cross promotion between our two businesses.

Ironically, and completely oblivious to Christi's text to me, my wife Kathy had reached out to Christi via social media to inquire about her interest in expanding her business into a second location, as she was the REALTOR® on a commercial building being constructed in the Downtown Bryan area.

Christi then explained that she and Tyson were already investing in multiple locations in the Northeast and were actually looking for someone to take over the current location. Very intrigued, my wife and I met with the couple to become acquainted, discussed the specifics of the business as a whole and the potential opportunity for us to jump in and be the new owners. As we sat through the discovery phase of the franchise, I noticed the very tight business model. It was attractive. Several shortcomings in my current practice were brought to light from stepping into another successful business model. A number of little tweaks made substantial impacts on our revenue, our productivity, and our culture.

Even in the "mastery" of my business and the success I had already achieved, I was willing to admit there were still things I was able to improve. It's a humbling feeling, but the moment you shut yourself off from learning is the moment you stall your growth. We are now the owners of that HOTWORX franchise location and have transformed ProActive Chiropractic into a new and improved model of its former self. It was already planned prior to this venture that ProActive would eventually franchise into multiple locations. Getting a behind-the-scenes look into another successful franchise allowed me to alter our franchising model on a more systemic level. The details blueprinted for that expansion provided much clarity for how I needed to incrementally and tediously execute my plan. Each phone call with corporate and our new mentors produced notes I used to streamline the ProActive franchise model.

Our timelines told us when certain events should occur and how one endeavor would snowball into the next. I had to preface and construct those timelines with questions that needed answers, especially upon reaching each milestone in our growth. A business plan is good, but it's useless if you don't actually utilize it. The only problem is that you can't utilize it if you don't ask the right questions in the first place and plot a correct course. We talked about the importance of connections. Surround yourself with an abundance of first mice that have found themselves caught repeatedly in the trap in their pursuit of success. Learn from their mistakes and allow yourself to thrive because of it.

My business plan called for hiring an associate upon three years of being in business. This is when I anticipated being able to support another doctor in the office. Upon hiring an associate, I took the same Dr. Robin approach: interview thoroughly to be fully confident in who would fit into my business and my dreams.

During the interview process I'm both the first and the second mouse. I'm the first mouse because I face a risk—do I mesh with and trust the applicant? I'm the second mouse because I've learned from my predecessors' mistakes to minimize my own. I'm all about providing like-minded people with jobs, but not at the expense of my own. Then no one has a job.

I will not sacrifice all I have worked hard for and throw a contract across the table to someone I know nothing about upon our first-time meeting, I don't care how enticing you are. I know what I am looking for and to avoid ending up in the trap, it is solely my responsibility as the second mouse to not repeat those mistakes. Interestingly, because I'm offering my experiences as learning points to my new hire, I'm also the first mouse. See how that works? This is succession.

It's a privilege to get the opportunity to be the first mouse, so don't waste it. Take pride in playing the role to benefit an aspiring individual. That's what this whole book is about! This is one giant first mouse point of view to aid and assist you in becoming the best second mouse that you can be. I would not be writing this book if I didn't want to see you succeed in whatever your dreams are made of.

Even if you take my idea and blow it up ten times greater, I am honored to have inspired that. Be generous with your knowledge and share it with those who are willing to receive it with grace. I want others around me to be successful, even if that means they surpass my level of success. Never overlook the importance of being a good steward for those to come, enriching their lives by bringing awareness to the mistakes you've made. Proceed with confidence, never arrogance. Cement your legacy with a view of "I can do it" rather than "Only I can do it."

Breaking the Cycle

The second mouse's lifelong experiences condition him with both positive and negative responses to various situations. It's positive when we learn what and what not to do. It's negative when exposure to the first mouse is absolutely toxic. We can learn what not to be and what not to do from anyone. Some of the most difficult experiences can produce the most beneficial and pertinent lessons that carry us through future experiences. How we process these situations in our brains determines our success in overcoming negative stimuli. How will you allow these negative situations to wire your brain's responses to these stimuli? It's time to rip apart and rewire the negative hardwiring programmed into your brain.

Up to this point, I've painted a picture of my father as a well-respected and hardworking man. While the latter is true, the lessons I learned through the faulty wiring instilled by my father throughout my childhood have left me with many issues that, unfortunately, followed me into adulthood.

In the summer of 1994, leading into my seventh-grade year of school and the first year of tackle football, my father taught me the ever-important skill of angle tackling. The lesson, however, came from his response to my *inadequacies*. On this particular afternoon, my father called me into the backyard to "make sure I'm ready for tackle football." I was trapped alone with him within the confines of the privacy fence surrounding our backyard.

He and all 300+ pounds of power stood along the back of the fence with an already intense look on his face. I stood by the back porch with the football in hand, anxious about what was about to go down. He hollered across the yard, "You're going to throw me the ball. I'm going to start jogging at an angle to my right. I want you to take a good angle of pursuit, put your head on the outside, wrap up, and drive through me."

Sounded easy enough. Reluctantly, I threw him the ball and he began his route. I then proceeded to take my angle toward my target, positioned my head to the outside and BAM!

As I started to extend my arms to wrap him up, he violently threw his forearm, which left me flat on my back on the ground, gasping to catch the breath that had just been knocked from my body.

"I need you to bring more intensity!" he said.

I thought to myself, *I'm 135 fucking pounds! What do you mean bring more intensity?*

Every following rep resulted in the same outcome, me laying on my back looking up at this asshole standing over me, clearly aggravated and disappointed in me. With each encounter I became more and more timid, as I knew I was going to get trucked. The more timid I appeared to be, the more frustrated he became with me. After this process repeated itself seven to eight times, he had enough and said, "Fuck this! Switch me places!"

Well, this can't be good. I started my way to his former spot at the back of the yard. As I turned around, my father was already within 10 yards of me and closing distance quickly. His eyes were wide, his teeth were clenched, and he shovel passed the ball in a "think fast" manner. As soon as it hit my hands, he blasted through me with excessive force. I can only imagine from a third-person perspective that it looked like some demented cartoon. I fully left my feet upon impact and flew backward, smashing violently through the fence. I found myself once again laying on my back staring up at the sky, only this time I was laying in our back neighbor's yard on top of broken wood slats.

As I brought myself to my feet, I realized three or four pickets were nailed into my upper back. My father stepped through the opening of the fence, and without an ounce of grace, pulled the pickets from my back, exposing the numerous puncture wounds the nails left. At this point, I was just glad the *lesson* was over.

He then said to me, "Go inside, have Mom clean that shit up, and get your ass back out here. We're not done yet."

This was one of many similar interactions with my father that ultimately filled me with so much anxiety and insecurity. I was preprogrammed to respond to situations with emotionally irrational and violent responses. In real time, this was a nightmare. But somewhere in my future, I would understand that my father was teaching me how *not* to respond to these particular situations. We, as the second mouse, learn from the first mouse's mistakes.

Sitting in my condo in Kansas City 20 years later, my father randomly brought up that incident in conversation. He very casually said, "Remember that time when we were practicing football in the backyard, and I knocked you through the fence?"

I looked at him stupidly. "Umm, yeah."

"That was pretty funny, huh?"

I could not believe he just said that to me. "No! That was not funny." I don't know what was worse, the fact that it had happened in the first place or the delusion that somehow, in his brain, he thought it was funny. Such a traumatic and negatively memorable incident got laughed off as comical nostalgia. Earlier in the *Your Inner Circle* chapter, we talked about taking out the trash. No one has immunity from this. If someone in your life has become such a negative first mouse that it leaves lasting impacts and disrupts your peace, then you have to let them go.

I no longer have a relationship with my father due to continuous "fence incidents." One after another, I was torn down one "picket" at a time—quite literally. At some point, it had to stop. Now, there is a difference between forgiving those who are sorry and moving forward with them in your life versus removing those who will not contribute to the best version of yourself.

Only you have the power to unfuck your faulty wiring. You may already be hardwired for success, and that is great, but an overwhelmingly large percentage of our population are basically licensed electricians trying to rewire shorts in their circuits. This is sad but true. You've probably heard the saying, "It is easier to build strong children than to repair broken men," a quote some attribute to Frederick Douglass. That's true too. When you've been programmed via doubt and turmoil, you're either resilient to abrupt, negative stimuli and the fallout…or you're not.

Lapses in resilience from consequential responses have caused me an extraordinary amount of pain and misdirection. It caused anxiety so extreme that it manifested in poor judgment, multiple overnighters in the cop shop, hours and hours of therapy, and numerous addictions to cope with stress (a euphemism for PTSD). All resulted in learning how to move past paternal blame and rewire myself for success.

Are there times when I resort back to my initial wiring? Are there still moments when I respond like my father, the first mouse? Less and less, but yes. I remind myself that it's not who I am anymore. *You've seen what comes from these actions,* I tell myself, *so nip it in the bud.* It hasn't been an easy road, but bitterness serves no purpose. Not to sound cliché or cavalier, but you reach a point when you step outside the chains of the past, and no one can steal your joy. Obstacles removed are obstacles conquered. I've managed to break a generational cycle, not just for me, but more importantly for my own children.

The entire point of mentorship is having the ability to relay instruction to your successor with clarity, while having credibility in your instructions through your modeled actions. For example, I will never tell my second mouse to do anything I haven't done or that I'm not willing to do myself. Mentorship is a derivative of experiences worthy of being passed down to the next generation.

Are there any upsides to the indoctrination of a "Do what I say" upbringing? Yes, because second mice eventually cycle into first mouse roles, meaning we dip our toes into the unknown. Perhaps we take that step to become new business owners after years of working for the man. Perhaps we become first-time fathers or buy a home for the first time, or pursue a seemingly unreachable degree. Then we use second mouse insights to be a better version of a first mouse. Our words and actions can uplift and shape as we teach. We teach our second mice to become successful with the "power of because" approach. This approach validates the reason for your "Do what I say" instruction and is much more likely to get a favorable response.

For instance:

When you're taking patients back to the treatment room, be sure to document the specific criteria because we need to be insurance compliant.

Son, the reason you're grounded is because we instructed you to keep your GPS tracking on for your safety. Because you chose to ignore this, you caused your mom and I to worry and broke our trust, therefore resulting in two weeks with no phone or vehicle.

I need you to look people in the eye and shake their hand firmly when you're greeting them because this shows confidence.

When you're angle tackling, your head goes on the outside. Otherwise, you'll end up arm-tackling the ball carrier and most likely end up missing the tackle completely.

See the difference in the approach? Every learning opportunity is a growth opportunity.

At some point you transition from the coach to the player and pass the torch. This is succession. It leads me to one of my biggest fears in life; that I will not be the best first mouse for my children and end up sending them into adulthood with the same issues that I've worked so diligently to overcome. You cannot dwell on your past experiences and allow tunnel vision to cloud your judgment. It is imperative that you identify how you're currently wired. If your mind isn't set up for success, then get to the root of it and fix it. Take what benefits you learn and trash the rest.

CHAPTER 14
THE MIC DROP

Go confidently in the direction of your dreams.
~ Henry David Thoreau

As I write my conclusion, I sit here, poolside on a ship, sea breeze in my face, headphones blaring the Rudy soundtrack on repeat, drink in hand, somewhere in the Gulf of Mexico, and I reflect on everything I've shared with you. The shopping cart, the dopamine response, tips on enticement, problem-solving, perspective-objective, passivity, your inner circle, living by the "C," overcoming obstacles, running to daylight, the story of the first and second mouse. All have led to this mic drop moment.

Be you!

Go out and apply all that you've learned, but always remember one thing: be your authentic self! Do what you love and love what you do. That will make for success.

Never stop working towards your success! Never be misguided by pessimism, denial, self-consciousness, or the unconstructive "Count the tallies in the loss column." Remember, winning is a mindset. It is your time. You're next in line. Be the obscure anomaly that, with positivity and the implementation of productive habits, will soon be discovered in whatever realm you wish. Never give up on yourself, and never give up on your dreams. Mediocrity is the complacency of never chasing your dreams.

Keep sight of what success is. Do not lose perspective of what it is to be winning. Success is a state of mind. Winning is not necessarily determined on a globally objective level but rather a subjective journey. Winning is determined by the achievement of personal goals, the development of strong and successful relationships, finding the wins in your losses, and the promotion of personal growth. You must remember that it's never going to be a walk in the park, nothing is going to be handed to you, and most people are going to try to pull you back. I've encountered a lot of bullshit throughout my life, and while some I was dealt, some were definitely self-inflicted, but I have never stopped and refuse to give up. I will also never victimize myself because becoming successful is that much sweeter when faced with and overcoming adversity to get there.

Remember, there can only be a single richest person in the world. There can only be one strongest or fastest. There can only be one home run leader. There can only be one GOAT. Each field currently has only one industry leader.

When you're working your way through every obstacle that life is throwing in your face, you must ask yourself, "Am I fighting for something or against something?" Are you playing offense or defense? If you're not enriching your own life and the lives of those around you, then you're working against something. Success is not about convenience and selfishness. Success is about fulfilling your life through gratitude and meaningful relationships with those who align themselves with congruent principles. Always be moving towards achieving your goals. Fighting against the obstacles in your life is a negative mindset and will prevent you from ever overcoming those obstacles.

It's about finding the sweet spot! Finding the sweet spot is the continuous pursuit of perfecting your craft (discussed in the Dopamine Response chapter). When you find the sweet spot in life, you're completely at peace, and things just fall into place. It's the zone of optimal performance.

For the past several years, I've been putting pen to paper and adding countless contributions to what we have here today. At first, these were just ideas, but after a while, the book began to take shape. I was deep into the endeavor when life essentially told me to take a step back. Life began to pick up, the kids were all now in school, and consequently, sports and extracurriculars. My business grew faster than I alone could keep up with, along with moving houses, marriages, babies born, and multitudes of other stressors that made the book take a backseat endeavor.

I was all right with that because it allowed me to live. It also gave me the chance to breathe. I wasn't pedaling inorganic content to water down the pages. I wanted a genuine, heartfelt connection with you, the reader, and I felt the only way to do that was to take a step back and listen to life.

The knowledge we seek and the wisdom we share cannot be confined to a particular page total. Just remember to always jot them down, always keep your thoughts organized and always be planning your next step. Find what motivates you and keeps you disciplined. Live every day knowing that someone is watching you. Whether with admiration or envy, they are watching. No matter where you are in your life, you're someone's influence, someone's role model, someone's hero. You're always someone's hero.

Go out into the world with the eager persistence of the first mouse and the acquired wisdom of the second mouse. Remain steadfast in your well-thought-out, strategic, and heartfelt decisions, as you're confident in the items that you have loaded into your shopping cart. Never let the weight of each brick in your stack outweigh the foundation that rests beneath it. Always be a problem solver, as obstacles will continuously appear at your doorstep. Recognize these obstacles through an optimistic lens, with the perspective that we will become successful by conquering whatever is put in our way. Open the door and greet obstacles with a confident smile and a winner's mindset, reminding them that you will not be dethroned as the king.

Go live by the C and let the passive money streams pour in around you. Build up your empire with great enticement and surround yourself with the greatest supporting cast, all while showing gratitude to those who supported you along the way.

You are the successor.

ABOUT THE AUTHOR

Dr. Jason Allen emerges as a dynamic force in the realm of self-help and motivation. As a chiropractor, business owner, entrepreneur, devoted husband, and loving father, he brings a unique blend of professional expertise and life experiences to the forefront of his writing.

Raised in the heart of Texas, he developed a resilient spirit and unwavering work ethic that laid the foundation for his multifaceted career. Beyond the clinic, Dr. Allen is a visionary entrepreneur who has successfully navigated the challenges of business ownership. Balancing the demands of a thriving career with the responsibilities of family life, he seamlessly integrates the principles of leadership, discipline, and love into his daily routine.

Made in the USA
Coppell, TX
20 October 2024

38948169R00125